The God Academy

A Master Class in the Power of Attraction

Angelica Crystal Powers

Big Box Books

Library of Congress Cataloging-in-Publication Data
Powers, Angelica Crystal.
   The God academy: a master class in the power of
attraction / Powers, Angelica Crystal
ISBN-13: 9781461193975
1. Success in Business—Religious aspects.   2. Success—
Religious aspects.   3. Wealth—Psychological aspects

Library of Congress Control Number: 2010910126

Printed in the United States of America

2 4 6 8 9 7 5 3 1

Big Box
Books

To all the future graduates of the academy. And to Oprah.
You were right.

Contents

The Disciples of Akrah

Introduction

Acknowledgments

I WISH TO EXPRESS MY HEARTFELT LOVE TO MY students who have prodded me to produce this work. For years, I was convinced it could be irresponsible of me to unveil the powerful wisdom of Akrah outside the circle of a selected list of clients and handful of closest friends. My own spiritual mentor, who had just turned ninety-five years old, convinced me that the ageless wisdom in this book is too important, too powerful not to share. He showed me another path, and revealed to me that, like a dragon guarding a pile of gold, I was hoarding riches that were never really mine to begin with. To that great teacher, Sri Swami Katananda, may you rest in peace. You slew my dragon.

The Disciples of Akrah

ACCORDING TO LEGEND, OVER TEN thousand years ago, high-ranking delegates from the nomadic tribes of the ancient Middle East assembled at the headwaters of the Tigris River in the Caucasus Mountains to elect an elite committee of mystics to carry out a singularly sacred duty. They were charged with protecting a priceless piece of oral tradition, an anthology of the most powerful and esoteric body of wisdom ever produced by humankind—the analects of *Akrah*, collectively known as the *Akranah*. The lessons of this manual described, in detail, spiritual technology developed for the mastery of living an unconditional life, from the secrets of attraction to the keys for love and unlimited wealth. In short, it described how one might elevate oneself from mere human to god.

Each of the nine delegated priests was assigned a single lesson, described in a thousand quatrains of verse, to protect and pass on. In order to ensure that no single priest carried in his memory the Akranah in its entirety they were, however, denied any knowledge of the contents of any of the other eight lessons. The Akranah was thus protected from falling into the wrong hands.

This elected coven of spiritual masters, the disciples of Akrah, known collectively as the *Kakranah*, or "Carriers of God," were instructed to act not as missionaries intent on conversion of the masses, but as educators, disseminating their wisdom among the worthy, regardless of wealth or social standing. These itinerant priests were protected by a symbol of nobility in the form of a unique insignia branded into the palm of the left hand. Once presented and the priest identified, members of any tribe encountered were expected to offer food, shelter and protection. In exchange, the Kakranah would share their wisdom and enlightenment. For generations, this arrangement proved fruitful and ensured a lasting peace and prosperity for all.

As tribes grew larger and the struggle over land and resources intensified, some tribal leaders came to the consensus that the central tenet of the Akranah— the proposition that anyone wishing to become a god could do so—was potentially destructive to the established political structure. Together, these rulers organized a small posse of assassins trained to identify and eliminate all nine members of the Kakranah, their very existence erased from the annals of history.

Fortunately, the dispersed and fragmented analects of the Akranah survived in the oral traditions of the Fertile Crescent's disparate tribes. The image of Akrah, no longer spoken of openly in public, found its way into later mythologies. Its masculine and feminine aspects were converted into the male Enlil and the "Mother Goddess" Inana of ancient Sumeria. (Inana later became Ishtar of Babylon, then Anat in Canaan, and then Isis in Egypt.) Aspects of the Akranah are still present in the sacred literature of many of the world's religions.

What remains conspicuously absent from these derivative mythologies, beginning with Babalonia's *Enuma Elish*, is the Akranah's core message: Every person retains the power to become a god. The claim that this concept has been purposely expurgated from Occidental religious texts and dialogue remains unchallenged; the Western religious tradition, in particular, is characterized by the idea that God and human beings are irreconcilably separate.

Despite all efforts to limit access only to the most powerful members of the ruling class, the ancient wisdom of the Akranah survives to this day as poetry occulted within the prose of our most familiar volumes of religious philosophy, encoded within the great art, literature and religious texts of the world. The great wisdom of the Akranah remains hidden, but it is hidden in plain sight.

Deciphering this message, however, is no easy task. In a text decoded from a fragmented cuneiform tablet, the ancient Sumerian mystic, Eannantumtum, foretold of a number of texts that would emerge to reveal the message of the Akranah to anyone with the desire to receive it. The following classes represent the first attempt to bring that prophesy to fruition. For the first time in history, the dispersed pieces of this ancient curriculum have been reassembled into a single text, this guide, this map, this way of life—the book you now hold in your hands.

Introduction

IF YOU ARE ONE OF THE HUNDREDS OF apprentices I have guided over the past decade who have been blessed with the knowledge contained within these pages, then you already appreciate the power of the secrets of the Akranah to bring the kind of unlimited success that transforms a person's life. For you, the following pages will serve as a single-volume reference, a compendium of the nine sacred lessons of the Akranah. So many of my students had, over the years, requested that I create this book that I felt compelled to complete it. And now that it's finally finished, I am especially grateful for those students' unremitting encouragement and insistence.

If you have yet to be introduced to these concepts, however, you may still be struggling to achieve the success you desire, and finding it all the more frustrating knowing that people who have taken control of their destinies are all around you. You see a golden light flickering through the window of a 10,000 square foot ski lodge, knowing that some couple is likely sitting next to a roaring fire following an afternoon of attacking the slopes, and you wonder, *Why not me?* As you move through the first-class cabin and elbow your way down the aisle and wedge yourself into your coach seat, you say to yourself, *What makes the people up in first-class so special?* Perhaps you've been fortunate enough to have been flown to some exotic locale for a corporate retreat and marveled at the confidence and charisma of the keynote speaker, someone whose own business has just enjoyed another year of phenomenal success and asked, *Why aren't I up there on that stage talking about the success of my own business?*

If you understand and practice the secrets of the Akranah, then you are already doing what you want to do. What you deserve to be doing. You are fulfilling all the richness and splendor of your destiny.

If, however, you have yet to be introduced to these powers, then allow me to offer you a heartfelt welcome. You are the intended recipient of a gift that has travelled for thousands of years to deliver itself to you. And you are the subject of my passion, the open-minded seeker compelled to reach out to probe the outer surface of the possible. You are an incipient power quivering at the edge of a radical transformation, about to travel down a path of infinite possibility. This is a path I have come to know well. As you follow this ancient path, it will sprout to life at the touch of your footsteps, its flowers blossoming at your feet.

Along the way, please know that, no matter the challenge you might be feeling, and the current state of your life, you can learn to harness these powers and use them to enact a radical transformation. When my spiritual quest began over a decade ago, my life was in shambles. I had taken a risky step and abandoned a life of affluence, and before I knew it I was clinically depressed, overweight, and my health was falling apart. Important relationships slipped away. And my credit card debt was mounting by the day. I felt unlucky and sorry for myself. I sometimes felt cursed, convinced I was paying retribution for some unspeakable sin I had committed in a past life.

All this suffering, however, was necessary. I needed to hit rock bottom before I considered that, before I could get my life in order, I needed to get my spirit in order. So I sold everything I had left to travel the Middle East, Europe, China, Japan and the mountains of Nepal and India on a three-year spirit-quest, a journey that ultimately led me to some of the most amazing and powerful spiritual teachers in the world, mystics of Akrah as well as spiritual guides from other disciplines who, I am so grateful to be able to say, considered me worthy of receiving their wisdom. The knowledge I was exposed to throughout my spiritual journey felt as strange and foreign to me as the many countries I had visited—each a place with its own language, customs and rules. Soon, however, I came to realize my soul had been waiting to return to that territory of knowledge, the true homeland of every spiritual being, all along.

After studying with these masters, I still had no intention of becoming a teacher myself, let alone a Master of Attraction dedicated to carrying on the ancient tradition of the Kakranah. Not until the final leg of my journey, in northern India, did this change. There, in the holy city of Varanasi, I met the man who would become my mentor and guiding light, the venerable Sri Swami Katananda. He told me I had been blessed with a rare ability to understand the concepts of the Akranah, and to communicate those principles to others. He helped me understand that with one's unique talents comes an obligation, a duty to make use of those gifts. With his encouragement, I began the second part of my journey, the journey of a teacher, a guide through the ever-expanding landscape of the divine.

As your guide into this foreign territory, I will on occasion speak to you in the lexicon of the great mystics, the vernacular of the sublime—the language of Akrah. I mean to share with you elemental truths that lie far beneath the reach of words and language, realities that flow through energetic strata far beyond what the ordinary tools of algorithm and argument can apprehend, revelations accessible only to the poet, the artist and the mystic inside you. You must trust your ability to dance with these truths until the steps become second nature.

Some of the concepts in the following lessons will not just challenge your beliefs; they will test the limits of your comprehension. So be patient with the material and, more importantly, with yourself. Understand that many of the world's greatest mystics have spent years trying to comprehend *any one* of these concepts; only a small, elite group of mystics can be said to have mastered them all. With this in mind, please read and reread every chapter *in order*. Underline what resonates with you and make notes in the margins. Make this book your personal journal of discovery. But most important, be as the growing vine reaching toward the sun until it finds a lattice to climb upon: *Move in faith*, and keep reaching toward the light. Trust that soon enough, with the guidance of Akrah, the lattice will be there, and you will climb up into a world where your dreams will spontaneously materialize.

Many of those who have attended my seminars or studied with me as personal apprentices have described what it felt like to abandon their previous realities and step into the full luminescence of Akrah— to earn and receive their diplomas as graduates of The God Academy. Having, years ago, made this same journey myself, I can tell you that the leap into this void of light can make you feel suddenly unmoored and weightless. This new knowledge can elicit sensations bordering on the surreal, like learning how to breathe underwater or lift a car without effort, or discovering that—if you turn windward and extend your arms just so—the slightest breeze will lift you into the sky. If you're not used to having your desires spring from the ground and roll up to your feet, this newfound power can even be frightening. The first moment of flight brings with it the fear of the possibility of falling, which, for many, is simply too much to bear. Some of us would rather choose to keep our feet firmly on the safe ground, living a life that, though less than fulfilling, is at least familiar.

We are right to feel a certain sense of danger at the beginning of any grand adventure, but I suspect you already know intuitively that refusing to accept the challenge is a far greater risk. When the skills you will learn from the following classes begin to transform your life, they will feel like magic, because they are magic. These classes will reacquaint you with reservoirs of power within you that are currently laying dormant. The prospect of awakening the powers of your inner god is nothing to take lightly and, as we'll discuss later, should be considered carefully. As you expand and revise your consciousness, your universe will be expanded and revised. As your consciousness is rewritten, so too will your universe be rewritten. In order for your consciousness to be reborn, a part of you will have to be left behind, and you may find it difficult to recognize your new, more powerful self.

Consider the monarch butterfly leaving its cocoon, drying its wings in the warm breeze and finally taking flight from the height of a milkweed plant: Any metamorphosis is necessarily frightening. But it can also be exhilarating! Take the leap knowing that this momentary fear is a small price to pay for a life renewed.

What if you are not yet ready to open the door and walk into this new life? What if you rub the lantern and a genie emerges and offers to fulfill not just three wishes but all the wishes you desire, and the offer is so overwhelming that you find yourself tongue-tied, unable to respond? If this happens, don't be concerned. If you feel unprepared to receive all the dreams your imagination can produce, that's okay. You can return to the life you've always had knowing your spirit will wait for you. At the very least, you will know more about why you have chosen the life you have elected to live. And you can take comfort in knowing that a life of magnificence, fulfillment and unlimited abundance awaits you if you decide to lay claim to something more.

Whatever path you choose, the nine ancient lessons in this book will help you to resist judging yourself and the people around you. The universe is an intelligent system of dynamic energy of which you are an intrinsic and necessary element. If you decide to make the fullest use of these lessons, expect to wake into an entirely different world, a world characterized by a new set of emotional frequencies, rich colors and intense sensations—a world without limitation. Expect to be changed. But rest assured that this new world will recognize and welcome your soul as a vital spirit of love and gratitude interacting with the harmonizing energies of the cosmos.

You will not be heading into this new reality alone. You'll have a guide. I will map out the landscape of this world lesson by lesson. Once a graduate of The

God Academy, you will walk the thoroughfares that connect the visible world and the world of the eternal creative force, a kind of causeway system that allows gods to move freely from the material world to the numinous, nonlocal field of the divine, and back again. As a traveler of this system of passageways, you will have become a god incarnate, able to recognize other gods who, like you, chose to live a sacred life here on earth, and continue daily to choose to live that life to the fullest. These patient, loving beings—your fellow gods—have been eagerly awaiting your spiritual arrival since the moment of your birth. They *will* recognize you, embrace you, support you, teach and learn from you, and protect you as one of their own.

Love and faith, and no small measure of curiosity and a sense of adventure, have brought you here to this moment, to the marble steps of The God Academy. You are about to create a universe of your own making, one that, the moment your intention generates it, will seem to have existed forever because, in a matter of speaking, it has, if only as an ill-formed plasma of potentiality, like pixels on a screen waiting to be formed into a beautiful, perfect image.

As you exercise your new powers to manifest your desires, every person, every rock and tree, and every breath of wind that populates your creation will celebrate you as a master of infinite potentiality, an incarnation of god-consciousness springing out of the creative field in the precise form and frequency of you. You will have become the perfect marriage of the physical and the divine, you as you always dreamed you could be, a god in human clothing, dancing the eternal dance of the divine.

THE FIRST LESSON
The Law of Ego

The Law of Ego instructs us to expand the ego.
The essential problem with the ego, with our
shifting sense of self-definition, is not that it is too
vast, but that it is too constricted, too confined. A
restricted ego becomes intensified and
destructive, like sunlight through a magnifying
glass setting everything it comes in contact with
aflame.

Broadcast the warmth of compassionate ego
energy and let the circumference of your love
radiate eternally outward. Release the ego, and
take the whole of the universe in your arms.

"Think of a vast ocean filled with water on all sides. A jar is immersed in it. There is water both inside and outside the jar; but the water does not become one unless the jar is broken. What is the jar? It is I-consciousness—the ego."

—Ramakrishna

"The ego is simply the ignorance that limits the real Self to a single body out of a multitude of bodies, all of which are its own creation."

—Lakshmana Sarma

DEEP INSIDE YOU, A GOD IS PATIENTLY WAITING to emerge. In you sleeps the seed of an infinite being of pure consciousness and potentiality, a miraculous agent of the divine. You are the co-creator of everything you see and experience, weaving the fabric of the cosmos into existence. All your greatest desires hang ripe and heavy from all the branches of all the trees in all the world, waiting, *aching*, for you to collect them.

The moment you allow this reality to create a shift in your awareness, you will elevate your life into a realm where all the objects of your desire will be laid at your feet.

And what prevents us from reaching this mastermind of god-consciousness and aligning with the field of pure potentiality?

The answer is *ego*.

"Ego" can be defined a number of ways. Freud defined the ego as a kind of functional synthesis of the *id* (wanton, ungoverned lust) and the *superego* (the governing principle of mind, concerned with duty, responsibility and control). The spiritual concept of the ego, however, breaks away from the psychological definition. Under the Freudian interpretation, blind adherence to duty and responsibility, for example, is considered a function of the id's counterpart, the superego, the aspect of the psyche most concerned with ethical decisions. In the Buddhist tradition, adherence to duty is considered a function of ego and attachment, and it can, depending on circumstance, be considered an impediment to spiritual growth. Overcoming the temptation of attachment to duty was, in fact, one of the Buddha's three trials prior to his enlightenment.

It is the spiritual, not the psychological, interpretation of ego with which we are presently concerned.

Ego, in its spiritual aspect, manifests itself in two distinct, but equally destructive, ways. Think of these manifestations as two ugly twin monsters jealously guarding the riches of ultimate wisdom.

The first manifestation of ego is self-hatred, thinking you are unworthy to be a god; the second is self-aggrandizement, a narcissistic obsession with the costume of your material value.

If I were to ask you to imagine an egotistic person, you might envision a billionaire stock broker with slicked-back hair, or a politician with a smarmy smile, or a CEO on his cellphone berating his assistant as he steps down from his private jet. But there is another kind of egotist: the person who, rather than obsessing over what he perceives to be his extraordinary beauty, obsesses over what he perceives to be his extraordinary ugliness. Imagine Narcissus, but with this difference: Rather than falling in love with his own image, he despises it so much that he cannot turn away.

This spiritual notion of ego speaks principally to the habitual practice of object identification, of relating to oneself, to others and to all creation primarily at the surface level of the physical. Followers of Akrah believe that operating from ego-consciousness is not something to be judged as good or bad, but is instead seen as one of a number of available spiritual strategies. The masters of the Akranah make little reference to the emotional, spiritual and material costs that necessarily result from ego identification. This is because, although ego-consciousness is clearly limiting, we cannot assume that someone has not, consciously or unconsciously, chosen to limit himself.

Without first understanding the nature of ego, you will not be in a position to receive the full meaning of the nine lessons that follow.

These are the nine inhibiting belief systems typically associated with a person operating from a position of ego-consciousness:

1) *I am my money.* My value is commensurate with the total value of my possessions.

2) *I am my job.* I am defined by my professional advancements, my yearly salary and my position in the hierarchy.

3) *I am my physical body.* I am my height, or my good looks, or my waist size or my physical prowess. I am the number of children I have. I am the accomplishments of my children. I am my age.

4) *I am my reputation.* My value is measured in the currency of the assessments of others.

5) *I am separate from everyone outside my tribe.* Other people, other sexes, other races, other political groups, other religions, other countries, other species are my enemies. I have nothing to do with them. I identify with my family, my colleagues, my sports team, my religion and my country only to the extent that I have determined is in my best genetic, financial, professional or social interest to do so.

6) *I am my adherence to, or rejection of, my duty as I perceive it.* I am a team player, as I follow rules and authority without question, or I am a bad-boy maverick because I break rules and categorically ignore my so-called responsibilities. I seek approval from my friends and colleagues who share my posture toward duty.

7) *I must control everything, and everyone, around me.* Since I cannot trust the universe to provide for me, I will bend it into submission.

8) *I'm right, no question.* I am unwilling to admit other views, opinions and interpretations. This is the way things are. My way or the highway.

9) *God and I are separate.* I am the repository of sin, not a miraculous expression of divinity. I have no acquaintance with the divine. Any reunion I have with the divine creative force will happen, if ever, once my material body is dead.

Notice that each characteristic, which we will refer to throughout our lessons, can be applied to someone demonstrating what some would call an "over-inflated ego" *or*—this is key—to someone with a very poor self-image. We all know someone who exhibits these qualities, don't we? *Could such a person rightly be considered a miraculous manifestation of god-consciousness, or are they something else?*

The answer is rather complicated. A person living through his ego is a kind of doppelganger of his true, divine self, a false being who has temporarily taken the place of his true, higher nature. He is a god incognito, wrapped in the disguise of ego, someone who has worn his stage costume for so long that he now identifies with the mask, mistaking it for the self, losing acquaintance with his inner god entirely. In an effort to fill his insecurities and feelings of emptiness, he ceaselessly prowls for his next fix, be it money, sex, adrenalin, drugs, attention—anything to quiet the unquenchable desires that drag him through the muddy landscape of his appetite like a crazed pack of yelping sled dogs.

In an effort to avoid moments of stillness, the egoist must fill his days with a series of distractions. Like a chain smoker, each frenetic burst of chaos is linked to the next for, in silence, he risks hearing the voice of his higher self singing to him—his sacred being, *the voice of God*. To the person spellbound by his own ego, that sound, the resonant hum of the field of intelligent energy that underlies all visible phenomena, can be like sunlight upon a vampire's skin. The ego directs those under its spell to avoid this reconnection at all costs.

The primary problem with ego is that it separates us from God, from wading back into the bottomless primordial ocean of love and grace that creates and nourishes the world of material things, the ocean from whose waters every soul and every spirit of all creation takes form. Although our inherent divinity has the power to warm the fertile soil of all the planets in all the heavens, that inner seed of God, what some have called our "god in embryo," can sleep inside us for years on end, a seed locked in a frozen winter ground dreaming of growing out of the shadows to stand tall above an expansive forest of majestic, stately trees.

Of course, the conscious aspect of the egoist in love with his own reflection is too busy building an altar to his own image—his money, his car, his famous and powerful friends—to have any concern over his inner god. His material wealth gives rise to his happiness, rather than the other way around, and so when his material wealth leaves him, so too will his joy. Only when those riches dissolve, when his life unravels and his friends fall away, will he take the time to consider the reasons for his downfall.

The other egoist—the person who secretly acknowledges the folly of self-aggrandizement—is too busy carving a monument of idolatry and self-loathing, a fetish made of his feelings of inadequacy and low self-worth, and his failed compensations for that self-hatred, to have any interest in waking up his inner-god, his "god in embryo."

Ego necessarily involves an obsessive focus on the physical object of the self and the circumstances of a person's perception of the material universe, distracting him from his larger purpose. When the farmer falls in love with his plow, he neglects to till the soil, and he starves. The runner who obsesses over his new shoes trips and loses the race. This is how ego can bind us to the hulking weight of the material world.

The wholesale erasure of ego, however, is not the solution. The shell of the ego must be cracked open so that its interior can intermingle with the field of pure potentiality, allowing this underlying creative force to be accessed. This is the first step toward effortlessly manifesting the objects of your intention.

If you have not yet attained god-consciousness, it is not because your ego is too big. *It is because it is too small*—too constricted, too focused like a laser beam upon the tiny dot of your material reality and physical being. In this configuration, the ego serves as a vehicle of *exclusion*, shutting out joy and lightheartedness and exultation and nourishment—everything but the surface layer of the self.

Thankfully, the cure is simple: *Expand your ego! Release it!* Lay personal and spiritual claim over everything and everyone you see! Walk into every room as if you own it. If you see a beautiful sports car driving by, claim it as your own. Say, "There goes my car. I'm letting that nice fellow drive it." Know that you own every house you see, every motorcycle, every airplane in the sky. Why covet them, when they are already yours?

The great American poet W.S. Merwin wrote, "What you do not have, you find everywhere." Take inventory of all your property. Take pleasure in counting all your fish in your oceans, and your trees in all your acres of all the forests of your world. Love them; cherish them; defend them, for they belong to you. Smile at every doctor, teacher, policeman and personal trainer you meet. Be kind and supportive;

they are all your employees. Feel exultation for the blissful couple, the successful entrepreneur and the lottery winner, just as you would feel for your own children. These are the members of your family, players on the field of life. You are their coach, their god, and they look up to you. So act the role! Be not envious; be protective and proud.

One client of mine was trying to succeed in the world of high-end art. And although he held a Master's Degree in Art History from Columbia, he insisted that many of the most wealthy clients at the New York gallery where he worked seemed not to take him seriously. I recommended to him that, over the course of the next thirty days, he try to convince himself that he owned the gallery, as well as every painting on display. As he later revealed to me, he had taken my recommendation one step further. "I decided to believe I was the artist behind every painting, " he said, "and I took real pride in each of my creations." By the end of our thirty-day experiment, he had sold more paintings in that single month than he had sold in the previous year.

As I'll discuss later, one of the aspects of the *Law of Attraction* is that *you must behave as if you already own the objects of your desire in order for those things to gravitate to you.* What people sometimes fail to understand is that you must not limit your sense of ownership to those things alone. You must reach further out, allowing your intention—as well as your love and appreciation—to radiate into the farthest reaches of your dominion. As you meditate, or when walking on the beach or communing with nature in a quiet forest, visualize standing at the very center of stillness, of restfulness. Practice expanding the circumference of your intention and showering your energy in wider and wider circles, like a celestial gardener watering all the soil in the vast garden of the universe. Feel your intention crossing over ahead of you and into your future destiny, tending to the seedlings that will, in short order, produce all the fruits of your desire.

Do not limit your vision of desire to those things that you feel are "realistic," those things that you have calculated to be within the realm of possibility. Rather, dream for the "impossible." Make "impossible" your jumping off point. Identify the core of your most unrealistic, ridiculous, over-the-top dream, and then ask yourself, "What is it about this image, this dream, that I find most appealing?" Is it a spectacular home? Warm friendships? A perfect partner? Security? Self-empowerment? Confidence? Significance?

Of course, we all want all these things and more. But there is absolutely no reason to limit ourselves to those dreams that we feel we are "entitled" to—whatever that means. Dream with passion and faith and the universe will not merely manifest your desires but provide far more than what you had hoped for. Do not merely envision those things which you think might someday gravitate into your life but also those things that you've convinced yourself stand miles outside your reach.

In other words, *dream for a life you are convinced you do not deserve.*

Though we might mistake limiting ourselves as an act of discipline or humility, in reality this is a function of the constrained ego. Who are we to estimate our value and, in turn, our worthiness to receive the bounty of creation? And who are we to presume that, by enjoying our lives to the fullest, this will somehow diminish the lives of others? If you desire unlimited financial success and all that comes with it, then desire it! Bring these images into being! Then trust the universal intelligence of the creative field to govern your worthiness to receive them.

Do not destroy your ego. Release it! Allow it to ripple outward to embrace everything with the protection of your love, God's love. In the Akranah, this instruction is called *The Law of Ego*, because your consciousness, as well as the list of subjects that fall within the protection of your bliss and intention, must *include* all.

The ego is a wonderful thing, but only if you make the ego *inclusive* rather than *exclusive*. Expand your ego over the surface of all creation. Envelop the world in the warm embrace of your ego. Does your ego contain contradictions and inconsistencies and struggle and reconciliation and anger and forgiveness and love? Of course it does; it contains all. As a great poet once said, "[You] contain multitudes."

Without even realizing it, you have already attracted these lessons into your life. Your ego expanded and laid claim to this knowledge, and it became a part of you. It belongs to you as much as your heart and your liver and your arms and legs belong to you, this missive of wisdom whose sole purpose was to be sent across a vast expanse of time and space so that it might deliver itself to your doorstep.

A god's ego is infinite, because all aspects of a god are infinite. A god's ego is synonymous with the universe, and therefore nothing exists outside the boundaries of the healthy ego.

A god loves the universe because he loves himself; he is both the projection and the projector of love, whose ego is without boundary or circumference. A god cannot help but be mesmerized by the pure awareness of his own spiritual anatomy—the sum total of every one and every thing—because he has chosen to identify with everything that has ever existed and everything that will ever exist.

A god is a Narcissus figure falling headlong into the pond, becoming the water and then delighting in his ability to reflect the stars.

As a god, to love yourself is to love the world.

THE SECOND LESSON
The Law of Infinite Return

The Law of Infinite Return tells you to give that which you wish to receive. All things are drawn back to their origins. Positive thoughts and interpretations are returned to you through the positive thoughts and interpretations of others. Images of wonder and beauty return to their creators in the form of manifested desire. All physical projections of the field of infinite potentiality fall back into that same field, like waves crashing into the sea.

"As a mother even at the risk of her own life protects her only son, so let a man cultivate goodwill without measure among all beings. Let him suffuse the whole world with thoughts of love, unmixed with any sense of difference or opposed interest."

—Guatama Buddha

"Cause and effect, means and ends, seed and fruit, cannot be severed; for the effect already blooms in the cause, the end pre-exists in the means, the fruit in the seed....You cannot do wrong without suffering wrong."

—Ralph W. Emerson

THE *LAW OF INFINITE RETURN* IS SIMPLE. SINCE the energy of the universe is in a constant state of circulation and fluidity, everything returns to its place of origin. In the context of the *Law of Attraction*, discussed in a later chapter, the *Law of Infinite Return* tells us that we must give out what we intend to receive in order to keep the channels of good health and abundance open to ourselves and to those around us. When we give love and attentiveness and support, we receive love and attentiveness and support. When we offer discouragement and vitriol, we receive discouragement and vitriol. When we broadcast thoughts of illness and toxicity, we receive the same in the form of depression, stress and disease.

The *Law of Infinite Return* has been called many different things over the centuries: "the law of love," "the law of giving," "the law of circulation," and "the law of the great connecting river." But there is a crucial aspect of the *Law of Infinite Return* as it applies to your relationship with the dynamic creative force that is not often discussed. It tells us that, because we are all projections of the sublime creative field, that field is the place to which we must return.

Like droplets of water falling back toward the surface of a welcoming ocean—observing and reflecting and intermingling with one another—we are all projections of divine consciousness. The *Law of Infinite Return* states that, because the divine generative field is the source of our being, it is our destiny to commingle with it, again and again.

The big question for us human beings is whether to choose to postpone this reunion with the divine to the distant future or choose to reconnect with God today, right now, in the life we're living.

In the West, it is typically presumed that the return to this field of spontaneous creation, to God, will take place only after death, after we have shuffled off our mortal coils and moved on. To some followers of the Christian Evangelical tradition, the claim that we become one with God in this life, or even in the afterlife, is heretical. In the Old Testament of the Bible, the uber-masculine, personified sky god of war is depicted as a sort of insecure tyrant, willing to offer his love only after we have—on pain of an eternal hellfire —followed his mandate to love him first.

As evangelical writer Rick Warren describes God in his book *The Purpose-Driven Life*, God is obsessed with the calculus of love given versus love received, a miser jealous of His own power, doling out His love in measured proportion to the amount of time His followers spend on their knees in praise. Warren's is a god who "gets jealous and angry," whose endless insecurities are assuaged only when we human beings, "planned for God's pleasure...his benefit, his glory, his purpose, and his delight," spend our lives inventing new ways to worship Him. One could easily forget that Mr. Warren is referring to the source of all love and creation, rather than a cranky, passive-aggressive child with abandonment issues. The best-selling author goes on to remind us that the proposition that we are divine is an "old lie," that "earth is not heaven," and that "life is not about you."

Take that in for a moment: *Life is not about you.* Does this resonate with you? If so, then accept it as your truth. Now, in the alternative, try this: Life *is* about you. And it is about the people around you. And the bird landing on the branch outside your window. And the cloud that takes a certain form, then another, then another. And about the lichen that grows on the side of the rock that remembers the heat of the setting afternoon sun, the rock upon which you may now sit as you consider these disparate perspectives.

How we see the world, whether as antagonist or friend, largely depends on the perceptions of our parents, an outlook most of us adopt for ourselves unthinkingly. If a parent makes a habit of overreacting every time her toddler falls down, the child will take on that energy and soon learn to see every minor bump and scrape as a major catastrophe. If the parent obsessively fears microbes, this fear will return to the parent in the form of her child's obsession with washing her hands. If the parent's greatest fear is drowning, this fear will return to the parent in the form of a child who panics in the water, putting the child at risk of drowning.

Automatically accepting the secondhand perceptions of our past conditioning without question makes as little sense as wearing hand-me-down spectacles. Just because someone else's prescription helped to bring the world into focus for them doesn't mean it will work for you. In fact, it will most likely make your world more blurry, and you will ultimately come to accept that world as normal. A person's conditioning from fundamentalist parents, for example, trains him to see God through the prism of ego-consciousness. The egoist equates riches with character, and so his god is seen as a rich king wearing a bejeweled gold crown. The egoist is obsessed with hierarchy, and so God becomes the "supreme" ruler of the universe dominating his flock, completely separate from human consciousness. As this separation generates friction within the human/God relationship, to smooth things out, love for God becomes compulsory: *Love Me or burn in Hell.*

According to the teachings of Akrah, this egoistic view represents an entirely appropriate image of God—*if and only if this is the sort of god with whom you intend to enter a relationship.* One of the central tenets of the *Law of Attraction* is that our thoughts, feelings and intentions create the universe. If you envision a universe in which God is separate from you, a god who hoards the powers of intention and creativity for himself, then that is the universe you will create. If, however, you envision a universal life force whose overflowing love interacts with you directly, then this will be the god of your universe. The nature of your god—even whether or not, for you, God exists at all— depends upon your intention, with what you wish to return to you.

In his extraordinary book *How to Know God,* writer and speaker Deepak Chopra wonderfully encapsulates this truism of Akrah wisdom: "When someone asks, 'Is there really a God?' the most legitimate answer is, 'Who's asking?'" And so, when someone asks, "What sort of god do you base your spirituality upon?" ask, "Who's asking?"

To extend the question further, *Do you believe that, in your universe, you will have to wait for the day you leave your material body to be one with God, or might you initiate this reunion today, right now?*

Depending on the nature of the tradition you inherited from your parents or consciously chose for yourself, this question is the central defining feature of your personal tradition: *to be or not to be divine.* Of course, how we relate to this question—whether we question the particulars of our past conditioning or accept them indiscriminately—depends largely on how we have been taught to interpret our religious texts.

Before we discuss the power of interpretation of religious texts, let us take a moment to better understand the nature and function of the language of myth.

In the same way there is no "right" type of light to shine through a diamond, no "proper" way to hold a diamond in the light, and no one "correct" perspective by which to behold it, powerful religious literature is designed to be regarded from a variety of angles and perspectives. The stories and their symbols operate differently, depending on each unique consciousness with which it interacts.

What is true of our two-way creative relationship with the sacred is also true of the religious literature meant to illuminate the sacred, the interwoven network of the intelligent, orchestrating system of the cosmos and our never-ending interaction with it. The texts help to create and influence our intention, consciousness and perception. And our intention, consciousness and perception, in turn, helps to create and influence those texts.

> *And God said, This is the token of the covenant which I make between me and you and every living creature that is with you, for perpetual generations: I do set my bow in the cloud, and it shall be for a token of a covenant between me and the earth.*
>
> —*Genesis 9: 12,13*

Consider, for a moment, the nature of a rainbow. Though a bright sun shines down upon a light rain, a rainbow may not appear. What is essential is that the sun shine down at a particular angle that will reflect light to a viewer standing at a spot toward which the rainbow's light is shining.

Imagine seeing the most brilliant rainbow you've ever witnessed and, in your excitement, calling two friends to tell them to look out their windows before the rainbow fades away.

The first friend, who lives several miles away, tells you, "I see it! It's spectacular!" However, the second friend, whose house just across the valley is even closer to yours, insists there is no rainbow. "I don't see it!" she tells you. "Are you sure I'm looking in the right direction?"

Why would a rainbow appear for two of you, but not for the third? What if the friend who failed to see a rainbow was always the one left out in the cold, always left standing on her back deck in the rain while hopelessly searching an empty gray sky? Would she be correct to deny the existence of rainbows altogether, to become, in effect, a rainbow atheist? "I respect the fact that you guys see rainbows all the time," she might say. "But I've never seen one, so I can't really relate."

How could you and the friend who lives several miles away have seen the same rainbow? Were there, in fact, two identical rainbows, which just so happened to be appearing at the same time, in the same general area?

A rainbow is a phenomenon born of a relationship—the relationship between the sun, the veil of rain falling from the sky and an observer. Though the sun moves across the sky and the rain clouds pass overhead, and we the observers move from place to place, the same rainbow can continue to be witnessed, as long as the specific angles—the relationships—are maintained. Two people can admire the same rainbow, appearing as though viewed from the same place, even as they stand miles from one another, because they are participating in the same relationship.

The *Law of Infinite Return* helps us to understand how witnessing the rainbow corresponds to our relationship to God. In the metaphor, the sun is the light of the divine, the rain is the physical world and those looking into the sky—some who see a brilliant bow of color and some who see only gray—are us. The inclusion of the rainbow in The Flood story in the Old Testament serves to remind us that if we find ourselves shut out from a relationship with the divine, it may well be the result of our failure to move from our position, our insistence that, because we cannot see the rainbow from our back step, it must not exist. We deny the existence of beauty and, lo and behold, the sky is filled with nothing but gray clouds.

More than this, the *Law of Infinite Return* advises us to place our focus more upon our relationship to the divine than upon the individual participants of that relationship. In reality, we are defined, more than any other thing, by the relationship we choose to maintain with the divine and our willingness to behold its gamboling panoply of light. As you peer toward the sheets of rain showering the distant hills, hold still long enough to see past the gray skies and into the technicolor horizon revealing the face of God.

The *Law of Infinite Return* tells us that, through our intentions, we send out a prayer to the dynamic creative field requesting God to appear in the manifestation we choose, typically in a form we find familiar and comforting. If yours is a god who is loving, and expansive, and generous, then send out your desire with deep intention and feeling. Your desire will be provided for you. If your intentions are born of bliss, joy and infinite possibility, then you will be provided a god of bliss, joy and infinite possibility.

If, on the other hand, your intentions are colored with the hue of anger, spite, bigotry, ignorance, jealousy and judgment, then—in less time than it takes to rub a rusty lantern—this is exactly who appears, a god of anger, spite, bigotry, ignorance, jealousy and judgment. In reality, since the ever-giving, ever-responsive force of God is not bound by the the rules of the temporal world, your god has already donned the clothes of whatever form you desire, long before you ever desired it.

It follows, then, that any example of great religious literature, like a great cathedral awaiting the arrival of our blueprint so that it may construct itself, is also dependent upon the intentions of the person reading it.

Very often I encounter students who have difficulty thinking of their most cherished religious literature in this way. One student in particular, whose father was a well-known televangelist in Mexico, had been raised in an environment in which a rigid, doctrinaire interpretation of biblical scripture was insisted upon. The student was particularly troubled by the story of Noah and The Flood. If this story is to be taken literally, then God indiscriminately killed thousands of people, choosing only to save one man, his family and a stable of animals. This was something my student felt was irreconcilable with the image of a merciful and loving god.

His father's acrimonious view of the world had returned to the son, confusing his son's interpretation of this familiar Biblical story, which had leaned progressively toward a preference for a god of love, peace and forgiveness. I suggested he look away for a moment from the literalist interpretation, and instead focus on the positive metaphorical message. The story of The Flood, as I explained, is one of a ritual cleansing and ablution of the accumulating sin that had, over the years, stained the region. The Flood, like baptism, is meant to represent a sort of washing away of sins, a rebirth into a divine forgiveness and grace. The value of our discussion was to help this young man understand how the energies of his father were circulating back to him. And not just in this one instance, but in several aspects of his life.

Many of my students have been victim to this same predicament. They understand the relationship of our perception to the physical world—how, to borrow a phrase from physicist Brian Greene, our intention causes physical reality to "snap out of the quantum haze and take on a definite value." But they sometimes think that religious literature is somehow exempt from the same powerful effects of their intention. *It's already been put on paper in black and white,* they protest. *How can my personal reading of it affect its content?*

Rather than approaching the literature with an open mind, they instead read with the intention of confirming what they have come to understand as the appropriate meaning of the literature, trying to imagine the writers' original intention so they can read the scripture "correctly."

This is a dangerous approach. Without proper instruction, more often than not we wind up bringing to these works the second-hand interpretations of others—a minister, a friend, a parent or some other authority figure from childhood. Rather than allowing the texts to live, we press them into the limited configuration of another's personal intent. Rather than remaining supple, diaphanous and luminous, the pages grow bone-pale, turning brittle and opaque as the leaves of a houseplant forgotten in the corner of a dark and musty basement to wither and petrify.

As we'll discuss in the next chapter, the true magnificence of the best religious writings rest in their receptiveness, and responsiveness, to interpretation. Like the protean, flowing, dynamic field of creation to which these writings refer, great mythical texts quiver and shift in anticipation of the reader's approach, ready to open whatever doors he or she is willing to walk through, whatever world he or she is prepared to experience. If one intends to enter a world in which Jesus Christ will return with a sword of violence and retribution (the more prosaic interpretation), then that unforgiving sword is placed in Jesus' hands. If one sees the sword as an instrument of love, as a blade intended to cut through the suffocating chains of ego (the more poetic interpretation), then this is the instrument now placed in Jesus' hands.

The *Law of Infinite Return* tells us that whenever you broadcast your personal interpretations of the divine into the cosmos, you must expect those interpretations, and all their consequences, to return to your doorstep.

The image you send out is the image that boomerangs back to you. The power of intention turns your perceptions into realities. The solidified forms of your interpretations, as they are reflected back to you, confirm your interpretations of the world, whether good or bad. This is the *Law of Infinite Return* at work.

Let me tell you a story concerning the power of interpretation as it applies to Infinite Return. Are you familiar with the Robert Frost poem, "The Road Not Taken"? As you may recall, it ends with these lines: "Two roads diverged in a wood, and I— / I took the road less travelled by, / And that has made all the difference."

I remember, years ago, touring the executive offices of one of my clients and seeing an inspirational poster quoting those famous words, and my long-time client, the owner of the company, said to me, "Angie, do you know this poem? *I took the road less travelled by, and it really did make all the difference!*"

He was mainly referring to the fact that he'd sold his startup software company just two weeks earlier for tens of millions of dollars—the reason he had generously flown me in for a celebratory dinner party that evening. By his interpretation, the poem was a joyful meditation on the rewards of acting independently for the sake of independence. He hadn't considered the possibility that the poem might be one of regret.

"So, 'don't follow the crowd', that sort of thing?" I asked.

"Right, exactly! Go your own way!"

"I like your interpretation!" I said.

My friend was taken aback. "What do you mean, 'interpretation'?" he asked, furrowing his brow as if I had just ripped his poster from the wall. "Frost was saying that he had the guts to take the road less travelled by and he's glad he did because everything worked out great!" he insisted.

After a moment, I turned to him and asked, "Was he?"

Every day that my friend read the words on the poster, he sent his interpretation—his intention—into the poem, until the poem, framed on the wall, was infused with that frequency. Other people in the office, operating in sync with their boss's vision, had come to see the poem in exactly the same light.

I truly did appreciate his view of the poem. My point was, and is, that our interpretations of the world —all facets: poems, events, religious literature—are a form of intention, which have the power to gravitate those intentions back to us, and ultimately to the people who surround us in the form of manifested realities.

Consider the power of interpretation in our daily conscious experience. The light from distant stars takes years to reach us. And so the night sky, as we see it, is but an interpretation of the celestial neighborhood as we understand it to exist in present time. Every thing you see and feel takes a fraction of a second for your brain to process, so the world you experience, in a very literal sense, no longer exists. Seen this way, we understand that our unique sensory experience is no more than a pragmatic interpretation of the most utilitarian of fantasies, the dream that best facilitates our daily interaction with the material world.

We benefit by harnessing the power of interpretation, and by taking responsibility for that power. We are not beholden to our interpretations; they are beholden to us. Your perceptions are mere tools for your use, lenses you can either borrow from others or grind yourself to make sense of the journey of your experience. You can dispose of, or modify, or exchange these lenses to fit your needs. These lenses of perception not only dictate your interpretation of the world but also intensify and focus whatever intentions you broadcast into the universe.

Think of the extent to which the authority figures in your life—whether external or internalized or invented—have molded, and continue to mold, your perceptions of the world. You very likely belong to the same political party as your parents. You probably share the same religion, eat the same kinds of foods. You may even live in the same part of the country, though you have dreamed of living elsewhere.

All these things, all these habits, serve to reinforce your perceptions.

Perhaps you vehemently rejected your parents perceptions, deciding to go the opposite direction, to create your own set of counter-perceptions as a kind of antidote to the more disagreeable world views that pollute some of the experiences of your childhood. Understand that even your "new and improved" perceptions refer back to the ones you have chosen to reject, and are therefore forever linked to them. They are, in a sense, molded by them.

There is no getting away from this: Your past is part of you. It does not, however, control you.

Imagine how the night sky must have looked to someone hundreds of years ago whose authorities insisted that all the stars in the sky were equidistant from the earth, like pinholes in a backdrop of black felt just beyond our reach. What strange creatures, do you suppose, were permitted to inhabit the bottom of the ocean in this person's state-sanctioned image of the sea? And how might this person have viewed himself, given that he lived under the rule of people who would deliberately place limits on the wonders of the universe?

Although we may not readily acknowledge it, our perceptions largely depend upon the whims of those who wield influence over us. Like stuffing whales into tea cups, the powerful sometimes have the habit of trying to cram our world into whatever dimensions best suit their personal agendas. And why would these authority figures choose to take such advantage, to leach all the power and mystery from the universe? Why would people use their power to build a wall between ordinary people and an overwhelming experience with the sacred?

To this question there are two answers. They did so because they were greedy and single-minded in their quest to acquire property, power and a sense of importance.

They also did so because, in effect, we asked them to. We asked them to shield our eyes from the brilliant image of God until the moment we could feel strong enough to remove the blinders ourselves. We asked them to force us to earn our acquaintance with divinity, and they indulged us.

We might be tempted to think that, because of modern technology and all the information available on the Internet, we have been freed from seeing the world through borrowed perceptions and hand-me-down interpretations. These days, it is all too easy for us to become convinced that our interpretations are entirely our own, that they are the best of all possible interpretations.

A certain degree of resolution in our convictions is a good thing. But when we become convinced our interpretations are complete and infallible, we are indulging one of the aspects of ego. We feed the monsters of egoism, which dutifully guard our greatest desires so that we may not have access to them. These twin monsters are doing exactly what we request of them every instance we choose to operate from the center of ego-consciousness. Living from a center of ego while being surprised that your desires are kept from you is to be shocked as you watch those two monsters grow larger by the day—the monsters of fear and desire, of obsessive self-loathing and obsessive self-adoration—even as you approach their cave, head bowed, with a bowl in your hands filled with yet another meal for them to eat.

Do you believe that, in your universe, you will have to wait for the day you leave your physical body to be one with God, or can you initiate this reunion in the here and now? Do you suppose that your answer might be bound up with someone else's interpretation of the religious texts you hold most dear, or are you willing to approach these texts on your own?

These questions reach to the very core of the teachings of Akrah. How you answer will determine whether you are prepared to step out of your provisional self and fully break into blossom, to step into a world in which the boundaries between desire and realization dissolve away, or if you intend to stay where you are.

Within you sits the key to becoming one with God, and the power to attract wealth and success so effortlessly that onlookers will call it a miracle. The *Law of Infinite Return* tells us that our interpretations return to us in the form of objects, events and phenomena. It also tells us that, since we are all spiritual beings, as surely as rain finds the sea, your energy gravitates back to the expansive reservoir of creation, where it will once again commingle with its energy, to initiate the spontaneous manifestation of material realities. Will these be negative realities of failure and despair, or will they be positive realities of bounty and success?

This all depends on what you wish to be returned to you.

As we will explore further in the next chapter, you needn't put off your reunification with God, the universal creative principle. In fact, *in messages encoded in the world's great religious texts—including the opening pages of the Bible—you have been invited to do precisely that.*

THE THIRD LESSON
The Law of the Dancing Symbol

The character of the symbols and iconography of the world's great religious and mythological texts depend upon your interpretation. Like any other element of your universe, symbols are brought into being in the specific forms you elicit through your intentions. If you intend to use the symbols to build a wall between you and the field of divinity, the symbols stack themselves like so many bricks into an impenetrable wall. If, however, you would prefer those symbols to lead you to the field of infinite potentiality, then those same bricks lay flat and pave themselves into a road. Without the touch of your consciousness, symbols rest still and inanimate. Your intentions and interpretations bring them to life.

"You are what you are by what you believe."
— *Oprah Winfrey*

"Truth is too simple for us; we do not like those who unmask our illusions."
— *Ralph W. Emerson*

THE *LAW OF THE DANCING SYMBOL* IS ONE OF the most difficult concepts in the curriculum of the Akranah. We began to pierce this mystery in the lesson on the *Law of Infinite Return* as we discussed the power of interpretation to shape the universe, and how the images of that universe, in turn, feed back into our perceptions. Think of the *Law of the Dancing Symbol* as an extension of the *Law of Infinite Return*, specifically as it applies to mythological iconography and metaphor. *Infinite Return* is related to *The Dancing Symbol*, as all of the laws of Akrah are interrelated and interdependent. Now, we will take this concept of infinite return one step further. Here we will examine the symbols of myth, or archetypes, which operate as communal interpretations, shared lenses of perception that have emerged over the course of human history from the fertile ground of our collective unconscious.

You could say that enduring mythical symbols exist in the commonly held territory of all sublime systems of interpretation. It is the space where our most insightful and spiritual perceptions overlap and vibrate in perfect resonance and harmony.

The *Law of the Dancing Symbol* has been called "the Law of the Shifting Symbol" and "the Law of the Gamboling Hare." During my time in India, the mystic of Akrah under whom I studied explained to me the original meaning of the *Law of the Dancing Symbol*.

The Akranah tells a tale of a skillful hunter tracking a desert hare, which suddenly stops and bravely turns to face the hunter, standing directly in the hunter's path. The confident hare confuses the hunter, who stands stupefied and frozen. The hare then runs off, and the hunter pursues. When the hare approaches the edge of a river and jumps in, the hunter dives into the murky water after it and soon becomes disoriented. Out of the darkness a massive trout suddenly appears, staring directly at the hunter, startling him. In his moment of hesitation, the hunter loses sight of the trout, and swims back to shore. To his amazement, he witnesses the fish leap from the water and transmute into a great hawk that flies into the sky. When the hunter climbs back to the riverbank, fighting to catch his breath, he finds the hawk standing on a rock, waiting for him.

Before the hunter's eyes, the hawk turns into a man, who is also a god.

The god asks the hunter, "Why did you not throw your spear when I was a rabbit? Aren't you hungry?"

The man said, "I have been hunting these lands for many years, and never had I seen such a beautiful rabbit, fish or hawk. They seemed so proud, so noble, that I could not bring myself to kill them."

"But it was my intent that you should kill me. This is why I appeared to you as a perfect meal."

"Then why did you keep changing shape?"

The god furrowed his brow, as if the hunter were asking about something that should have been obvious.

"Because I didn't know what you wanted to bring home for dinner."

This idea of consuming the flesh of a god figure predates Babylonian times, and is still found in most of the world's religions to this day, such as in the Christian ritual of transubstantiation.

As I mentioned in the discussion of the *Law of Infinite Return*, the universe awaits our instructions—in the form of thoughts, feelings, intentions and perceptions—so that it can manifest from the quantum plane into visible phenomena. As the ancient story of the hunter and the "dancing" hare illustrates, the specific form our god assumes is responsive to our needs and desires. As I said earlier, if you wish to put the sword of retribution in Jesus' hands, then your intentions, as well as your interpretation of scripture, will place it there.

The *Law of the Dancing Symbol* tells us that the lenses through which we view God are not made of hard and brittle glass; they are fluid and dynamic and ever-changing. Too often, we mistake the archetypal image, the lens, for God, rendering the lens opaque and useless and shutting out our access to the field of infinite creation. This process turns the archetype into a kind of fetish or, to use Biblical terminology, a "false idol."

The *Law of the Dancing Symbol* tells us to allow all the archetypes of religion and mythology, including those to which we personally relate, to dance and shift in reaction to, and in accordance with, our intentions and interpretations. Allow these flexible lenses to reform themselves for your benefit, helping you to bring the image of the sublime into sharper focus. When you witness the divine, the field of infinite potentiality allows that image of God to flow into your life like light entering your eye. And the lens of perception must act very much like the lens of the eye, flexing and contorting so the world may stay in focus. When our perceptual lenses are stiffened by the rigidity of narrow-minded thought, we lose touch with (our vision of) the divine. You can no longer see the divine light glowing all around you.

It is time to allow the archetypal symbols to dance again, for the supple lens to be allowed to refocus until the fact of ultimate creation can once again come back into view. This is a never-ending process, a cosmic feedback loop of consciousness and spiritual energy. Although we are often willing to allow the lens to make minor adjustments, and for the symbol to slightly alter its own form, the inertia of our past conditioning often makes it difficult for us to allow the symbol to reform itself and roam as freely as it needs to—to dance. We find it relatively easy to make minor revisions in our spiritual outlook. It is far more difficult to undergo spiritual upheaval, to enact a radical transformation of consciousness.

To achieve this transformation, sometimes it is necessary to take a sacred mythological symbol and, in a sense, jump straight through it—to see it from the other side, free from the interpretations of others. Then we see the symbol for what it really is, a portal to the divine, not some leaden object blocking the way.

Think of the rabbit from the story, only now our rabbit is stuck, struggling in the thick tangleweed of centuries of the accumulated interpretations of others. *Release it! Set it free!* Then follow it over the hills and contours of your own spiritual journey, trusting the symbol to lead you to whatever it is you need to discover. Who knows where the symbol might take you, and what creative manifestations it might assume to serve as your god?

In simple terms, the *Law of the Dancing Symbol* reminds us that whenever a threadbare, shopworn, second-hand interpretation of our sacred symbols brings feelings of pain and confusion rather than those of joy, intimacy, comfort, peace and clarity, then we must allow ourselves to reinterpret those symbols a different way so that they may better serve us.

Most of us in the West are well familiar with the story of Genesis in the Bible. In the King James translation, Adam is warned by God not to eat of the tree of knowledge of good and evil, "for in the day that thou eatest thereof thou shalt surely die." Later, after Eve is formed from one of Adam's ribs, a serpent approaches her and says, "Ye shall not surely die: For God doth know that in the day ye eat thereof, then your eyes shall be opened, and ye shall be as gods."

(Later, in Chapter 6 of Genesis, the serpent's prediction is played out. These "sons of God came in unto the daughters of men, and they bare children to them, [and] the same became mighty men which were of old, men of renown.")

Then, as the story goes, Adam and Eve are summarily cast from the garden. To make certain that the couple would never return, God "placed at the east of the garden of Eden Cherubim, and a flaming sword which turned every which way, to keep the way of the tree of life."

Many ministers of the religious establishment are firm on their interpretation of this story: The serpent represents evil, the devil in disguise. Eve, susceptible as she was to the serpent's duplicity, earned women the punishment of extra suffering during childbirth, a reminder of her weakness and her inseparable kinship with the devil. The young couple was cast from the Garden of Eden because they had discovered the difference between good and evil. And mankind must never return because we need to be punished for man's "original sin," The Fall.

There is, however, another way to interpret these symbols. First, let us take a closer look at the various meanings of the tree of life and the tree of knowledge and their functions in the context of the Garden of Eden.

Consider for a moment that the Garden represents the shared consciousness of Adam and Eve. It is the physical manifestation of their intention. Since they cannot imagine a world outside the walls of the Garden, the Garden represents the world entire. God, too, lives inside the walls of the Garden, strolling about at his leisure and appearing in person to interact with Adam and Eve, then making himself absent when the serpent enters the scene so Eve and the serpent can discuss the fruits of the tree of knowledge undisturbed.

The world of the Garden is one of complete unity, existing outside the world of duality. Since past and future represent a duality, time does not exist. Right versus wrong is a duality, so judgment does not exist. Man and Woman represent a duality, so Adam and Eve do not recognize one another as different. Separate identities represent a duality, so Adam, Eve and God coexist as three aspects of the same being. Even the snake is part of this shared consciousness— with one key difference.

The snake can cast off his dead skin. Death, like its counterpart, birth, has no place in a world of non-duality. So what is the snake doing there? And, while we're at it, why does he speak only with Eve and not with Adam?

In mythological traditions around the globe, the snake is interpreted as a sacred being due to its ability to shed its skin. A snake shedding its skin is simultaneously alive and dead, with one foot, as it were, in the world of unity and the other in the world of dualities.

This explains the serpent's unique kinship with Eve. A woman, with her ability to give birth, represents this same miraculous ability to exist in two worlds at once, the world of mortality and the world of enduring life. During the birth process, the woman and baby represent two beings inhabiting a single conscious realm, fracturing down the middle; the emerging baby can be seen as a new life shedding the body, or the "skin," of the mother.

When you see the serpent and the woman as representing this wonderful concept of the universal field of unity (non-duality) sprouting into the local field of duality, you can see how Jesus also symbolizes this same concept of renewal. The Bible tells us that Jesus was the son of God, a culmination of a perfect god-consciousness in the form of a mortal man.

As with the literature of so many other religions across the globe, this concept of the eternal creative spirit in the clothing of a mortal body appears throughout the Bible. At the core of each of these symbols is a reminder that within you resides God-energy, God-consciousness, and a limitless creative power. They are all invitations welcoming you into the realization that you are a god.

To help insure we don't miss receiving this divine invitation, the story of the Garden of Eden leaves us with one more potent and inviting symbol: the guardians at the gate.

After Adam and Eve take of the tree of knowledge—knowledge of duality and the landscape of the material world—God becomes concerned. "Behold," he says, "the man is become as one of us, to know good and evil: and now, lest he put forth his hand, and take also of the tree of life, and eat, and live for ever." The King James Bible tells us that God "drove out the man." There is no mention, here, of Eve; her ability to give birth suggests that she was already well acquainted with the relationship of the material world to that of the field of infinite unity and abundance. God then "placed at the east of the garden of Eden Cherubim, and a flaming sword which turned every way, to keep the way of the tree of life."

Consider this story for a moment. God creates for Adam a woman, and then places a serpent in the Garden to "beguile" her into eating of the tree of knowledge. After she and Adam do exactly that, God says, out loud for all to hear, *I certainly hope they do not now eat of the tree of life while the flesh of the fruit of knowledge is still in their stomachs! He has become a god, like us! If he now eats of the tree of life he'll realize his true nature as an all-powerful god! We had better guard one of the many entrances to the garden with... cherubim!*

Cherubim is the plural of *cherub*, which the *Oxford Dictionary* defines as "a winged child or the head of a winged child," an adorable creature wearing the benevolent smile of the angel in Bernini's masterpiece *The Ecstasy of Saint Theresa.* Some Biblical scholars chafe at this warm and fuzzy image of the cherubim. They argue that a more accurate description of the cherubim of Genesis is somewhat more intimidating than a couple of smiling toddlers. To some, the guardians of the East entrance of the Garden of Eden are formidable beasts with four faces—those of a lion, an ox, an eagle and a man.

Which interpretation is accurate? Is the serpent of Genesis an enemy of God or, rather, his conspirator? Does the God of the Old Testament regret allowing Adam and Eve to tread so closely to achieving ultimate power, or did he deliberately articulate the instructions to achieving godhood out loud so that we might be compelled to comply?

If you can eat of the tree of knowledge and the tree of life in the same meal, and thereby hold within your consciousness unity and duality at once, then you "shall be as a god," an all-powerful being whose dreams are within your reach. Does the Genesis story invite you to do this, or does it insist that you follow a life of want and suffering? Do you envision the guardians of the tree of life as terrible monsters whose sole purpose is to bar you from happiness? Or, rather, are they children whom you yourself placed at the entrance to the garden, grinning infant angels whose only concern is the integrity of your intentions, and who are willing and ready to lower their flaming swords at your request so that they may lead you by the hand to the tree of life?

This is the beauty of the Dancing Symbol. The symbols of God take the shape that you desire, the form of whatever it is you most urgently need in your life. But they will do so only if you allow them to. If you wish to live in frustration and suffering, then the symbols will mold themselves to that desire. If you intend to reenter the garden and "be as gods," then the symbols will open up to that desire as well.

You can choose to be a god or you can choose to be a servant. You can live in a universe filled either with love or with hate. It's all up to you. The wonder of great and enduring mythological symbols rests in their capacity to dutifully break open and present both of their two aspects at your approach; which of the portals will offer passage into the myth depends entirely on your present consciousness and intent. Each symbol is designed to divide into two portals, two doors through which one may choose to step through and enter a spiritual reality. In this regard, a symbol is always bifurcated, a road diverging in a wood. Which path you choose will, of course, make all the difference.

Imagine each symbol, each portal, pulsating with alternating colors: red, green, red, green—God as antagonist, God as love, God as antagonist, God as love... Each of us must choose when to leap through the symbol and into the myth. How we time our leap depends entirely on what we wish to be our relation to the divine. If you wish to enter the myth through the symbol that makes the story, and your universe, smaller and seemingly safer, then enter when the symbol glows in the hue of the artifacts of that limited world: Jump when it turns red. If you wish to enter the myth through the symbol that makes the story, and your universe, larger and more wondrous, then wait until it glows with the hue of that universe: Wait for it to turn green, then jump through to the other side.

Which world is for you? *It all depends on what you want to bring home for dinner.*

THE FOURTH LESSON
The Law of Attraction

The central tenet of the Law of Attraction is simple: Like attracts like. Thoughts and emotions about the wonderful things you desire attract those things into your life. Thoughts and emotions about the terrible things you fear and despise attract those things into your life.

"Always bear in mind that your own resolution to success is more important than any other one thing."
— *Abraham Lincoln*

"If you have faith as a grain of mustard seed, you shall say unto the mountain, 'Remove hence to yonder place,' and it shall remove and nothing will be impossible to you."
— *Jesus Christ*

THE *LAW OF ATTRACTION* TELL US THAT LIKE attracts like. If you are consumed with negative thoughts, thoughts of failure and money problems and frustration, then this is what you will attract into your life. If you insist on projecting images of success and affluence and vitality, then this is what you will attract. At the core of the *Law of Attraction* is the *Law of Infinite Return*. The further you ascend into god-consciousness while creating the images of your intention—by including generosity and love in those images, or through deep meditation or lucid dreaming—the more powerful the currents of magnetism you generate, and the stronger the signal of attraction you send radiating out into the universe.

Once your vision penetrates past the superficial world of appearances and materiality and into the underlying stratum of generative power that gives rise to the physical world, you begin to understand the universe at the quantum level, a bubbling, swirling sea of energy and unlimited potentiality. This quantum membrane serves as the interface between the physical world and the unifying creative force that is God. The quantum realm is the fertile ground of creative expression where the organizing force manifests objects and phenomena, and from which these things are conducted into the world of the physical. In the Christian tradition, these same concepts—the organizing force, the material world and the quantum realm—are represented by God, the son and the holy ghost.

According to our current understanding of quantum science, the laws of cause and effect, linearity of time, past and future and other aspects of duality dissolve as they approach the level of the quantum. In the quantum universe, particles cannot be said to exist or not exist in any one particular state or location. Rather, quantum particles behave more like clouds of potentiality, which await the intervening agency of a specific frequency of energy to direct them into one quantum state or another. With this direction, this catalyst carrying a specific energetic signature, the quantum cloud can then "snap out of the quantum haze and take on a definite value." It is these shifting configurations, these fluid and dynamic currents of quantum energy and the resultant quantum configurations, that ultimately give rise to the visible phenomena of our daily lives.

The quantum universe is extremely unstable, and each particle state is highly susceptible to influence. These influences can come from the field of infinite bounty and love—the field of God—or from the physical universe. Every thought you have influences this quantum field, which responds instantaneously.

People who have attracted wealth and affluence into their lives are filled with thoughts of wealth and affluence. Those who struggle with finances wake up with images of money problems filling their heads, negative images of unpaid bills and stagnation in their careers.

Whether or not you intend it as such, every image in your mind acts as a sort of prayer, and the content of that prayer is broadcast into the universe. The universe—an intelligent, kinetic, interwoven network of energy—immediately begins to reorder itself to respond spontaneously to your request.

Where are these images made manifest? It all begins in the quantum field, where quantum energy coalesces, by the magnetic power of attraction, around the seed of your image. Every element of quantum energy sits quivering at the head of an infinite number of pathways of possibility, its vibrations moving up and down an infinite vibrational band like a radio tuner moving up and down the frequencies looking for a new signal. And your intention acts like a radio station broadcasting the songs of your dreams and desires. If your intention vibrates at a higher frequency —of love and bounty and gratitude—then that particle of quantum energy matches this high frequency. If your intention vibrates at a lower frequency—of isolation and scarcity and bitterness and regret—then that particle takes on this lower frequency instead.

Out of an infinite number of possible paths, the particles of energy that receive and resonate with your desires open up the one path that matches their received frequency. As they travel along this fresh conduit, these particles orbit the image of your desire, protecting it like a swarm of bees ushering their queen to a new nesting site. The stronger the feeling of your desire and the deeper your investment in the image, the more quantum energy is roused into activity, and the more jealously your desires are guarded as they are ferried toward the local, material plane, where they take form.

At this point in the process, your desire, encircled by more and more quantum energy, is not physical, not even in the quantum sense. It is merely a singularity, an infinitesimal seed, a point of attraction—in the terminology of complex systems, a "basin of attraction"—pulling toward it all the quantum energy that now resonates with the specific tone of its own quantum signature. These energies orbit your image, feeding off one another in sync like an electric current locked in a magnetic field, until the seed of your image organizes the energy of quantum potentiality into one of the various objects of solidity and mass that populate the world of form.

This is the process by which the *Law of Attraction* operates to shepherd your intentions into the field of visible phenomena.

In order to make the Law of Attraction work for you at its highest possible level of energy, you must understand three key precepts:

1) The responsive powers of attraction operate in the quantum field, which does not contain or recognize elements of duality. In the context of Attraction, there is no difference between a positive proposition and a negation, nor between a wildly ambitious desire or a humble one. The generating power of any intention is dependent only on the emotional intensity, clarity and conviction of the image.

2) Intentions born of the higher god-consciousness are, by orders of magnitude, more powerful than intentions born of ego-consciousness.

3) You can manifest only that which you can dream.

Let us explore each of these aspects of Attraction in order.

Don't think of a pink elephant! Don't imagine it wearing a party hat! Did you think of a pink elephant wearing a party hat? What about an imperative containing a negative: *Do* think of a gymnasium in which *there is no* pink elephant wearing a party hat. Or think only of an empty gymnasium where a pink elephant was recently but is there no longer. Do you see how, in your mind, though the gymnasium is empty, the elephant's lack of presence still fills the space of your image? Maybe this will work: Imagine a pink elephant wearing a party hat and then imagine it disappearing completely. No more thoughts of a pink elephant, right? Or is that pesky elephant still hanging around?

Try another experiment: Think of a dark green elephant that loves you. It wants only to lift you with its trunk upon its mighty back for a nice walk down a jungle path. It strolls you through patches of dappled sunlight and as you progress farther down the dusty walkway, the muscles of its shoulders working beneath the weight of your body, you notice that the elephant has gotten smaller. It continues to get smaller and smaller until it is the size of a tiny mouse. This elephant-mouse then climbs into the palm of your hand and skitters up upon your shoulders. It wants you to carry it back up the path, for it is now late afternoon and growing cold and dark, and it is time to return for dinner.

Elephant, no elephant. Big elephant, tiny elephant. Since imagery operates primarily at the level of the unconscious, all the previous images have equal power. Your warm feelings for the elephant remained unchanged throughout the story; who is carrying whom is incidental. The unconscious mind operates with the same software employed by the intelligence of the quantum realm, software which admits no aspects of duality or separateness. In the field of the quantum, there is no distinction between an image or the negation of that image, nor is it influenced by the size of the objects of any given image. In the quantum universe, what differentiates one image from another, one desire from another, is the relative wattage of the broadcast signals it receives. And that "wattage" is determined by the clarity, specificity and emotional intensity of each image. All images, all thoughts, all the peculiar objects of emotional expression share equal value. Like an encoded message sent from a radio tower, the substance of any message has no effect on how far it will reach. What differs is the intensity of the broadcast wattage, the power of the image's carrier frequency—the passion and intensity of the emotion with which the objects and images of the desire are sent out into the cosmos.

Given these realities, you can see why it is so destructive to imagine what you fear, as you necessarily attract into your experience the objects and phenomena of that negative emotion. And you can understand why it makes little sense to dream small. The vast creative field does not recognize, let alone reward, the pragmatism of your dreams. It reacts only to the intensity and conviction of your desires.

The lingua franca of the generative field, its currency, is that of emotional value, emotional intensity. The generative field understands, and responds to, passion—an image of desire delivered with intensity. Whisper your dreams, and the universe says, *Huh? What?* Shout them, and the universe leaps to its feet. So if you're going to dream, *dream big!*

If you are a golfer, you already have some understanding of these principles. You step up to the tee and begin your pre-shot routine to drive the ball down the fairway, when you notice a large pond pressed up tight against the right side of the fairway. As someone prone to slicing, you think to yourself, *Whatever you do, just don't slice!* The image of a ball curving through the air inexorably destined to fall from the sky into a silent splash of water enters your mind, and the emotions of embarrassment and failure put butterflies in your stomach.

Any golfer knows how destructive negative images can be. Try as you might, you know the intrinsic nature of the unconscious, how it will register the image of a ball slicing to the right, which leads to the swing that produces this very flight. And so you try to shake the image off: *Don't think slice! Don't think slice!* Then, when you can't dissolve the image, you decide to settle for the image of a relatively minor slice, something more innocuous—a "power fade." You imagine the ball turning, ever so slowly, from left to right in the air and landing safely on the right side of the fairway, several feet away from the water.

And what single image from this internal conversation does the subconscious register?

A slice.

And what does the unconscious mind produce?

A wet ball.

Imagine walking into a room and discovering a large, mean-looking dog you are meeting for the first time. The dog looks up at you as if to say, "Now what? Are you afraid of me? Am I supposed to bite you?" And your subconscious responds by producing an image of the dog biting you. You can almost feel the pain of the bite, your pulse throbbing in your hand...

When, as if by magic, your image is realized: The dog bites you.

As I suggested earlier, the unconscious realm and the world of quantum manifestation operate on a similar set of principles. The images the unconscious mind receives and catalogues into memory are the very same images the quantum field receives as generative missives. Neither is receptive to whether you mean to reject the image or engender its fruition, and neither is

receptive to the size of the objects of the image. Be it desire or fear, both realms respond only in reference to the *emotional power* of the image.

The Akranah explicitly instructs how to harness the power of the *Law of Attraction* to manifest your desires. First, understand that the power of your thoughts and images is not a function of the positive or negative value of those thoughts and images; images of feared events and images of desired events have equal capacity to be realized in the material world. Buy a raffle ticket with the clear image of losing out on the Hawaii vacation, and you can be sure that you will not win. Bitterly predict that the person at the next table will win the vacation, imagine him stepping to the front of the room to receive his prize and returning to his congratulating friends, and this is the reality you could help to create.

This is not to suggest that powerful imagery will allow you to win the lottery, or any other contest of "random chance." Rather, the *Law of Attraction* suggests that, to use the raffle example, if you dream of visiting Hawaii, and you broadcast that desire with a sense of passion and certainty, then, in short order, you will find yourself walking on the warm sand of a Hawaiian beach. It may not happen as the result of the raffle drawing, but it will happen. Just remember: When it comes to attraction, specificity matters. If the image of your desire is specifically about Hawaii, then this is the experience you will attract. But if you send the signal of a more general image—of palm trees, white sand and limpid blue water—then it is just as possible you will discover yourself on a plane heading to the Bahamas, or Greece, or even some destination you hadn't even considered.

When students ask, as they often do, whether or not it is *literally* true that you create your own reality with your thoughts, I answer with this: *Each thought and intention creates a space that the corresponding reality may now inhabit.*

The one thing the self-proclaimed lucky and the self-proclaimed unlucky have in common is that both know, intuitively, that their lives are shaped and characterized by a preternatural governing force, and that this source is internal.

Both know that, in time, their thoughts will become things.

Only a fraction of these people, however, recognize that they are the generative source of their powers.

Have you ever had a day that just seemed to get worse and worse until you were almost afraid to imagine what else might go wrong, because every time you did, the terrible thing actually came to pass? You were not predicting events; you were manifesting them. These downward-spiral days are displays of your extraordinary powers of attraction at work. When you discipline your mind to produce only positive creative images (in the training ground of lucid dreams, which will be discussed in a moment), you will begin to have more days in which things progressively, and predictably, improve.

One story in the Akranah speaks of two competing gods, each of whom intends to create a world within the same open field in a forest. A third, elder god approaches to settle the matter. One god explains to the elder that he is convinced that he is the luckiest god in the universe and—so that he can enjoy his winning streak uninterrupted—should therefore be granted the claim. The other says he knows, with equal conviction, that he is the most unlucky god in the universe and that, given his misfortune, he should have equal claim. Every thought the lucky god has ultimately comes to pass. Every thought the unlucky god has also comes to pass. Each is powerful in his ability to form images intense enough to create the reality of his respective universe.

The elder god considers the matter carefully and says, "There is no issue here. You may both create the universe of your liking and lay one upon the other in the same field, and then both live within them. Your two worlds are entirely compatible and can exist in glorious harmony: The god convinced of his continuing good fortune will play the role of master, while the god convinced of his misfortune will be his servant."

Conduct yourself just as you would if you were already in possession of the material thing which you are demanding, when you call upon your subconscious mind.

—*Napoleon Hill*

Several years ago I was giving a seminar on the *Law of Attraction* to a group of advanced students in Maui. One of the students was an Olympic bronze medalist in swimming who mentioned visiting the spectacular home of one of the people featured in the movie *The Secret*. She said how impressed she was that this person's image of the exact house he intended to live in was so strong that, a few years later, he wound up owning the exact house he had originally envisioned.

I then asked all the members of the class to imagine their dream homes, down to the last detail. The point of the exercise was to discuss the power of specificity of desire; specific desires are more powerful and therefore more powerfully summon the powers of attraction. The students had no difficulty being specific, mentioning the makes and models of the cars that would be in their driveways, the Sub-Zero appliances and Italian granite countertops.

When it came to the Olympian's turn to describe her home, she began to describe an outdoor kitchen and dining room and a table at which all her most inspiring friends would gather to enjoy a lovely dinner. Her little brother had had leukemia when he was a young child, and so she talked about hosting families who would need a place to stay while their children receive cancer treatments in the renowned hospital in the city where she envisioned living. An animal lover, she talked about hosting grand dinner parties for the Humane Society and the A.S.P.C.A.

While most of the students talked about the physical objects that would occupy their dream home, she focused on people, on those whose lives she would be able to make more joyous once she had manifested her dreams of affluence. Because her intention was born of a higher frequency of her consciousness, immediately we all recognized the power of her vision, her god-consciousness.

As you attract your greatest desires, you must then allow this bounty to circulate into the stream of giving and receiving. This is key: These concepts of circulation, of giving and of gratitude, must all be included in your thoughts and desires as you broadcast your intentions. We must not presume we will be moved to share our bounty *after* we have reached the summit of success. The summit is illusory and always receding. Like the canisters of oxygen that sustain a climber on the ascent of a mountain, the spirit of generosity and gratitude must be taken with you *as you set out on your journey*, from the first steps leaving the advanced base camp of your spiritual adventure. This is what guarantees your intentions will be infused with divine power.

Within five months of that class, the Olympian phoned to tell me she had been offered a job in her dream city in California, and she had closed on the home of her dreams!

Stop the flow of blood, and your blood coagulates and you die. Dam a stream to hoard all the water for yourself, and you wind up with a pool of stagnant, mosquito-infested, undrinkable water. Let the currents of generosity and gratitude flow, and all the gardens of the world are fed by your aquifers. The *Law of Infinite Return* and the *Law of Attraction* represent two sides of the same reality. The first law speaks primarily to the circulating nature of perception; the second speaks to the circulating nature of intention.

Wealth-consciousness stripped of the desire to give as the primary motivator to achieve affluence sends only the faintest signal into the field of infinite potentiality. Though it may be received, or partly received, it takes very little for such a weak signal to be interrupted and fail to entice the powers of attraction and spontaneous creation into motion. You may never have put this thought into words before, but you already have a sense of the truth of this idea. If your dreams resonate with the lower frequencies of selfishness, vanity and ego, they are unlikely to manifest your desires. If, by chance, they do, then over time the products of those desires will certainly prove frail and ephemeral, their temporary realization no more than the overture to a long series of unfortunate events.

Over my many years as a life coach and spiritual guide to some of the most affluent people in the world, I have yet to meet someone who has been financially successful in the long term who didn't, throughout their rise to prosperity, intend to leverage their success for the purpose of making the world a better place. Whether or not the visions of these billionaires match yours or mine is beside the point. What matters is that they realized—some early on, some a little later—that their powers of attraction would harness extraordinary power, *godly* power, only when their desires included the intention to create joy for others. *Get rich, give rich; Give rich, get rich.*

The true joy of the acquisition of power is the ability to lift others into the aura of your bliss. A rare bottle of Lafite Rothschild Bordeaux is bitter to the palate unless shared with friends. A beautiful new sports car can be little more than a tin can of vanity, an ugly charm dangling from a rusty bracelet. But use that same car to drive someone in need of medical treatments to the hospital, and watch that car transform into a golden chariot. An opulent mansion with a stunning view can be a prison, a venus fly trap made of plaster and glass closing up around your soul. Fill that house with friends, throw a dinner party to raise funds for your favorite cause, and watch those walls blossom into a palace.

If you have yet to achieve your desires, then you can take solace in the fact that you are perfectly positioned to make the most efficient use of the power of attraction. Now is the time, before your dreams have begun to unfold, to interweave images of gratitude and giving with your material desires. There is no faking this, no loophole, no pulling the wool over the eyes of the divine. The divine is within you. God knows what you know. And what God knows, you know. From the outset, be committed wholeheartedly in your desire to share. Make this the central mast upon which you stretch the cloth of your material desire, then trust the cosmic winds of spontaneous creation to take you and your precious cargo to the land of your grandest dreams.

One of the minor books of the Akranah is called *The Book of Dreams*. The main point of that book is this: "That which you cannot dream cannot be manifested in your life." The title refers not only to the idea of dream as in "desire" or "imagine"; it refers more specifically to actual dreams, the kind you have when you sleep. The advice and techniques in *The Book of Dreams* can still be found in the literature of countless Sufi masters. The central lesson of this book is that dreams serve as the training ground for gods learning to fully harness their powers of attraction. But not just any sort of dreams—lucid dreams.

During deep meditation, we move further into god-consciousness. During dreams, you may or may not move closer to your god-consciousness. This depends on the whims of your imagination. Lucid dreams, however, allow you to take command of your dreams and guide them toward the light of god-consciousness. During lucid dreams, the images of your desires can be made so intense, so specific, so *lucid* that your power to attract the things you desire becomes limitless. In fact, if you can populate your lucid dreams with your specific desires, then manifesting these desires in your waking life will feel so effortless that it will seem little more than a formality.

The venerable Sufi teacher Jalaludin Rumi wrote, some seven centuries ago, "There is no cause for fear. It is imagination blocking you as a wooden bolt holds the door. Burn that bar...." Thoreau wrote, "Our truest life is when we are in dreams awake." If you consider both of these statements together, it becomes clear that the best place to learn to unbolt the door to our imaginations and unlock the potential of our "truest life" is while "when we are in dreams awake." That is, while we are in the midst of a lucid dream.

A lucid dream is a dream in which you realize you are having a dream. Once you learn the skill of "waking up" inside a dream, you can use your dreams as your personal training ground, self-directing every stage of your education as you progress through the curriculum of The God Academy. The trick, of course, is to free yourself from the leaden chains of past conditioning and guilt and allow yourself to experience anything your imagination can conjure up. Many people believe that, when a person fails to achieve spectacular success, this is more often than not the result of a failure of the imagination. The truth is, it is not your imagination that limits you; it is the fear of the prospect of your own imagination operating without limits. Anyone can imagine breathing underwater, or flying or enjoying a romantic encounter. The realm of lucid dreams offers a safe environment in which you can learn to give yourself permission to experience these things, to experience anything your creative imagination can produce.

This can be more difficult than it sounds. As soon as you experience your first lucid dream, you will learn how challenging it can be to allow yourself the freedom to experience your fantasies, at least at first. Dreams are worlds of your own making—every event, every experience, everything you see are the manifestations of your thoughts. During a lucid dream, all that stand between you and your desires are the internalized rules and strictures of your past conditioning. Your imagination can conjure up worlds experienced through senses you do not have in waking life. In the lucid dream, you can be anyone you wish. A single bird, or a flock of birds, or a flock of birds and the tree they have taken flight from, as well as the person watching this mass of fluttering color as it swirls and ascends into the sky.

In lucid dreams, you learn how unlimited your imagination is. But at the same time, you get a sense of how you may have been trained since childhood to deny yourself participation in the creation process your imagination is primed to set into motion.

Imagine you are in the midst of a lucid dream: You just realized that you are dreaming. You say to yourself, "I'd like to fly." You flap your arms a bit and begin to levitate into the air. Then you have a thought: "This is too great! Knowing me, I'll just get pulled right back to the ground." At the instant you have this thought, you are—just as you expected—pulled back to the ground. Since you can easily imagine what it would be like to soar through the air, what was it then that suddenly pulled you back? What was the source of this inexorable pull of gravity?

You already know the answer. You were pulled back to the ground by your own fear, weighted down by the insistent voices of limitation and contrition inculcated into your spirit by authority figures in your childhood. The authority figures that populate the memories of your childhood may have taught you these things with the best intentions, parroting the same rules and constrictions that the authority figures of their youth inculcated into them. And now those voices still resonate in your dreams, the voices of judgment and condemnation—the selfsame voices that now limit you in your daily life, and dare to invade your dreams.

The lucid dream is a place where you can act without consequence, a place of safety where you can allow yourself, like a rehabilitated wolf being released back into the forest, to take those first timid steps into a place of danger and possibility. In the lucid dream, you learn you are limited only by your capacity to fully commit to your belief, to have resolute confidence in your ability to manifest your desires. Then, you need only remove the leash of those confining voices of the past and release yourself into the verdant manifestations of your imagination.

How can we expect to manifest our desires in the waking life of the physical world when we cannot allow ourselves to unleash them in the context of a lucid dream, a world of our own making, a world without consequences, completely under our control?

The dragons that guard our rightful treasure must be battled and destroyed in our dreams before they can be battled and destroyed in waking life. The dragons are the same, but they are easier to destroy in the context of a lucid dream, where we are more willing to accept that our experiences are products of our own invention. When the Sufi master Idries Shah was asked to identify a fundamental mistake of a person unfamiliar with the realities of god-consciousness, he replied, "To think that he is alive, when he has merely fallen asleep in life's waiting room."

This is why Sufi mystics, Tibetan Buddhists and masters of mind potentiality throughout the world emphasize the critical place lucid dreaming holds in their spiritual teachings.

I recommend all my students get a copy of Dr. LaBerge's classic manual on lucid dreaming. But let me leave you with a few simple tips to get you started on your journey of mastering the lucid dream. Remember: If you can dream it—with intensity and specificity in the context of lucidity—then you can have it.

1) Set your watch to beep every half an hour. When it does, look around and say out loud the words, "Am I dreaming? How do I know? What is the evidence?" Then test your world. Look at written material and see if it looks normal. (When dreaming, letters and numbers often appear garbled.) Ask yourself where you are and how you got there. Remind yourself that if you're not

instantly certain you're awake, then you are in a dream.

2) As you fall asleep, tell yourself repeatedly that you will have a lucid dream. Say, "Tonight, I will realize that I am dreaming." Then establish one simple task to perform while in your lucid dream: Fly for a moment. Create a character. Or simply remain in lucidity for as long as you are able.

3) Focus on your intentions for your lucid dream. Imagine the specific scenario of the dream in which you plan to become lucid.

4) Stretch the boundaries of your waking life. Do unusual things, like wearing your slippers while walking around the block, or taking a nap in an unusual place. These exercises help open a channel of communication between the conscious and unconscious aspects of the mind.

5) On weekends (or whenever you can afford to sleep in), set the alarm a couple hours earlier than usual. Then go back to sleep. After several hours of sleep, the amount of time it takes to enter REM sleep diminishes. When you first go to bed, it takes an hour to an hour and a half to enter REM. By morning, it may take only minutes. If you focus on a lucid dream while falling asleep in the morning, the intention often persists all the way into the dream

state, at which time you can remember your plan to "wake up" in your dream.

6) Keep a dream journal. Make note of any consistencies in your dreams. Track the trends of objects or motifs that reappear. Perhaps the ocean shows up often, or riding in a red car. Maybe you often dream of being unprepared for a test. Then, in dreams and in waking life, any time you see or feel any of these dream markers, ask yourself, "Am I dreaming now?"

7) Don't give up. It takes at least a week or two before you can achieve even a few seconds of lucid dreaming. With practice, you can learn to experience lucid dreams almost every night you sleep. Then you can begin to engineer these dreams specifically to take fuller control of your desires and intentions, each time increasing their intensity and power. Lucid dreams allow you to bring your innate powers of attraction to a whole new level. Most important, when you are able to demolish the walls of limitation that hold you back in the context of lucid dreams, you will then be able to more easily demolish those same walls in your waking life.

THE FIFTH LESSON
The Law of Synchrony

It is easy to underestimate the power of synchrony. When a building or a bridge moves in sync with the frequencies of an earthquake, those structures are reduced to piles of rubble. When a ship moves in synchrony with the currents of water and air, it can sail around the world.

Moving in synchrony is to move with the rhythms and currents of the universe so that, like a surfer riding a wave, your efforts are multiplied to the point that very little effort gives rise to extraordinary outcomes.

"Sync is one of the most, if not the most, pervasive drives in all of nature. It extends from the subatomic scale to the farthest reaches of the cosmos. It's a deep tendency toward order in nature that opposes what we've all been taught about entropy."

— *Steve Strogatz,*
Professor of Applied
Mathematics at Cornell
University

HAVE YOU EVER GONE TO A RESTAURANT AND felt immediately that, for no reason you can easily explain, you didn't want to eat there? Or have you ever been invited on a trip or to a party that, for reasons you could not logically defend, every cell in your body seemed to be telling you to avoid?

When this happens to you, you are reacting to your intrinsic sense of the ebbs and flows of quantum energy, the currents of the cosmos. Your spirit senses that you are heading down a treacherous path and, like a sensitive horse bridling against the reins to keep you from taking her into brush in which a rattlesnake lies sleeping, tries to pull you away from the danger.

Why do we do things our hearts tell us not to do, even when our experiences tell us that every time we go against those instincts nothing good comes of it? More often than not, we feel an obligation to others, quite often presuming they want us to do something that, in reality, they do not.

When we indulge in this behavior, we are like a fish trying to swim up a waterfall, a rock struggling to roll up a hill. We are all familiar with this feeling: *I'm in the wrong place. I'm making the wrong choices. I pass up the easy, joyful path and head down the more difficult one, gritting my teeth, carrying the load that, as my programmers have assured me, will someday lead to prosperity. But now I realize I've been making all the wrong choices, never doing what I truly wanted to do. What if I've traveled down this road for so long now that I'm not me anymore, too far from home to remember who I really am?*

How can I hope to find my way back?

You find your way back by listening to the music of the cosmos and allowing your instincts to remind you to dance with the perfect harmonies of the universe.

If someone asks to dance with you, what are they really asking you to do? They're asking you to move in synchrony with their movements, to move to the rhythm of the music. But what if, as soon as you went out onto the dance floor, you decided to go against the flow of the dance and ignore any reference to the music or your partner? You wouldn't get to enjoy dancing with anyone else, jiving to the beat. You would find yourself bumping into other people. In fact, you might even wind up getting hurt.

The entire universe—every person, every rock and tree, every sunset, every moment, everything you see and everything you cannot see—is, at this very moment, inviting you to dance.

The swaying trees invite you to sway with them. The clouds request your company as they roll across the sky. The sun is lonely for its partner, the moon, and wants you to come rushing out your front door to join it, to run through the streets and chase it to the ends of the earth!

The traffic that blocks and then opens up. The flock of birds that settles onto the branches of the tree and then bursts into the sky. The great machinery that ploughs the field and drives the train and propels the ship and all the silly chitter-chatter of gossip and rumor skittering across the wires of the Internet—every last thing is now extending its hand out to you, asking you, begging you, to dance.

I am blessed to own a home on the Island of Kauai, Hawaii, literally fifty steps from the warm waters of the Pacific. Whenever my schedule allows me the luxury to stay there, I begin every morning with an ocean swim. Sometimes, when the surf is high, large waves pass over the reef and break across the entire bay, churning up five-foot walls of rolling white water. But under the waves you can see the green turtles and parrot fish and trumpet fish standing in the limitless blue, the ocean gently rocking them back and forth, back and forth, each as calm as a baby in its mother's arms. Their underwater world is playing music, and their bodies sway in sync with that music. They revel in it.

Hawaiian watermen and waterwomen watch how the creatures of the ocean behave, and they learn from them. Traditional Hawaiian thought holds that sharks and turtles and other animals are, in fact, protective deities, or *nā 'aumākua*. Time and time again, my Hawaiian friends give me the same advice about staying alive in the water: *Never fight the ocean!* Put another way, *Dance with the ocean, feel its rhythms and follow its lead.*

The *Law of Synchrony* deals with a kind of spiritual dancing, the dance of the higher self swaying with the rhythm of the cosmos. Letting your spirit move with, rather than against, the currents of creative energy will immediately benefit your life in the physical plane in ways that will amaze you. Once you learn to move in sync with the ebbs and tides of the energy of the universe in every interaction in your life, you will find yourself carried effortlessly to a place of astonishing affluence.

When you dance with the energies you feel surrounding you, you dance with the universe entire.

On a recent plane trip to New York, a handsome man in his late twenties was bumped up from coach into first class and was seated next to me. As it turned out, his sister worked for the airline, and he was thrilled to be riding at the front of the plane. We got to talking, and he told me that he had abandoned a lucrative business career and was now heading to New York City to be an actor. He didn't say he was going to try to be an actor. He said, "I am an actor."

He brimmed with joy and a humble, seasoned confidence, as if he had already achieved his dream. He wasn't going to be an actor someday. He *was* an actor. He knew it, and so everyone around him knew it as well.

He retold the story of his transformation of consciousness, the revelation that allowed him to realize his happiness did not depend on whether or not he would be a household name in six months. Once he was fully invested in his decision to follow his dream, the strangest and most wonderful things began to happen. First, he said, everyone around him seemed electrified by the energy of his joy and conviction, and they found themselves attracted to it. People who had previously been indifferent, even hostile, to him suddenly wanted to play an active role in his dream. They could feel his positive energy moving in sync with the cosmic flow, a kind of spiritual affluence, and they wanted to be a part of that flow, to be in sync with it. People he had only briefly met offered him places to stay in New York City, sending him contact names and numbers, anything they could come up with to help him manifest his dream.

Your instincts are like an array of highly sensitive equipment that allows you to detect the ebb and flow of the currents of the universe. When you open yourself up to those "gut feelings" and follow them, people instinctively sense you are operating in correspondence with nature's intelligence, and they immediately want to be near you to benefit from your sensitivity to the rhythms of energy. When people discover someone perfectly aligned with the magnetism of his desires, and with the infinite creative power of pure potentiality, they are drawn to him like people lost in a whiteout snowstorm huddled around the one person holding the compass.

People in sync with the powers of the universe recognize one another immediately, often forming powerful coalitions of shared intention. Consider the great scientists, artists, writers, inventors, explorers and entrepreneurs of history: Not one has achieved his dreams in isolation. In every case, these pioneers surrounded themselves with people of a harmonious energy and spirit, and all their dreams coalesced to form a nexus of attractive energy. The greater the number of harmonious intentions you surround yourself with, the greater the spiritual mass of your collective dreams, and the greater the concordant gravitational force attracting the physical manifestation of your desires.

When you surround yourself with people whose intentions are discordant from your own, then everyone's powers of attraction—like a number of musical tones perfectly out of sync with one another—are neutralized. In this cacophonous noise of competing energies, often the most negative intentions, which thrive on dissonance and chaos, win out.

In the worst case scenario, a self-centered person's energy will neutralize another's dreams and desires, and then commandeer their talents, their passions and their zest for new experiences. I have seen this happen time and time again: A person of average means marries up into a higher financial stratum, and then loses herself, her identity, entirely.

One client told me a story about an epiphany she'd had while putting the finishing touches on a monthly newsletter her husband had asked her to create for the members of his yacht racing club. She had learned to take great pride in her modest publication and in the compliments she received from her husband's circle of friends. But then one day she broke down in tears. She had realized that she was acting as a kind of mule, carrying the back-breaking load of her husband's hand-me-down dreams. Here she was, a woman with a PhD in literature, and all her time and talents were now dedicated to writing a competitive yachting newsletter. "I don't even like competitive yacht racing!" she told me. "Never have!"

The longer you forgo your own dreams to invest everything you have in the desires of another, the more you find yourself surrounded by the products of that pursuit. Everything you read and write, every conversation, every person you meet—all your daily experiences become more and more crowded with the objects of another's dream, populated with characters who move in sync with that person's energy, but not your own. Not only do you risk losing your sense of identity, but you also risk losing the close friends who might otherwise have helped you find the path that leads back to your own intrinsic nature and to the world that used to provide you so much hope, comfort and joy.

The danger of living inside the world of another's desires is that you can become like the worm living inside a horseradish. After a time, you come to believe that the whole world is made of horseradish, and you forget that you ever believed otherwise.

I once coached a couple who wanted to work on their powers of intention together, as a team. They had already achieved amazing success as restaurateurs in the Chicago area, but they felt their success had reached a plateau. And so they came to me for coaching on synchronizing their imagery. They explained to me how, months earlier, the financial advisor they had worked with for years had lost the bulk of their savings. Before this happened, they had been planning to move to Napa Valley to expand their restaurant chain, but this latest turn of events had, so to speak, put their dreams on the back burner.

After an extended session with the couple, it was revealed that the wife had long dreaded the idea of moving away from her family and her childhood home of Chicago. In fact, she had been praying, for months, that something would happen to prevent the move. And happen it did, in a big way. Only during our session did her husband learn of her resistance to moving. Had they communicated earlier—and brought their desires and intension into harmony—they could have avoided losing millions.

One student of mine was a rather overprotective husband who objected to his wife going downhill skiing because, years earlier, he had a skiing accident that severely damaged his knee. He warned his wife repeatedly that, if she continued to pursue her interest in skiing with her friends, she would have the same sort of accident he had and hurt her knee in the same way. He told her that he'd had intense, detailed nightmares about it. Interestingly, he felt strongly that *he* should continue to ski. As a businessman with a home in Aspen, he defended his choice to continue skiing on the basis of the idea that "the slopes are where the big deals are made." Every time his wife asked to accompany him, he repeated his warning: "You'll wind up hurting your knee just like I did."

And that's exactly what happened. Although she felt confident that, as long as she was careful, she could ski all she liked without incident, his image of her getting hurt proved stronger. She had an accident and injured her knee—same knee, same injury— exactly as he had predicted.

This story has a happy ending, however. After working with me for several more months, the couple learned to hone their skills of attraction, and to bring their powers into alignment with one another. They learned to act as a team, focusing on the image of the ligaments of their knees knitting themselves back together and healing. Six months after the wife's injury, not only had her knee fully recovered, but their orthopedist, one of the best in the country, said that both her and her husband's MRI scans showed no signs of the original damage. It was as if their injuries had never happened.

One couple actually came to me to learn how to *tame* the girlfriend's power of attraction. The couple was convinced that the woman's powers of attraction were actually *too* strong! They gave me a recent example of how her power had gotten them into trouble. Minutes before leaving for a two-week vacation to a beautiful villa in my home country of Italy, the girlfriend became so frightened of losing the $20,000 ruby ring her boyfriend had given her that she decided to hide it where no robber would ever think to look—pressed into a stick of butter in the refrigerator.

Only days into the vacation, her refrigerator back home suddenly died. So the woman's assistant kindly emptied all the rotting food, bagged it up and set it out on the curb in a garbage can. When the woman called her assistant to check up, she heard the full story, including the fact that the garbage had already been collected that morning.

Miraculously, however, only three of four cans had been emptied. The fourth, for no apparent reason, had been left untouched by the garbage collectors.

Upon her return, the woman and her assistant sifted through the stinking mass of garbage until, finally, they discovered, resting in the center of a melted glob of butter, her $20,000 ruby ring.

The man presumed the woman was so afraid of him proposing to her that her powers of attraction had generated a circumstance that would destroy this symbol of his love, the ring. But she insisted that this wasn't the case at all. They both agreed that she did seem to create this sort of chaotic event often—so often, in fact, that she nicknamed herself "Lucy," as in "I Love Lucy."

At the end of the session the girlfriend discovered that she was inadvertently attracting chaos into her life, and endangering her relationship with her boyfriend. She wasn't doing this for any malicious reason, and not for any lack of love for her partner, but simply because her loving childhood home was a place of constant chaos, and therefore she found chaos familiar and comforting. Her house was always under some sort of half-finished reconstruction, the yard and garden in perpetual flux. And so although her boyfriend sought peace and tranquility, her powers of attraction won out.

What did the chaos represent to her? Love. Acceptance. Attention. These are the things she really wanted. Ultimately, she agreed to stop worrying and attracting chaos if her boyfriend would agree to pay more attention to her and surround her with overwhelming, unconditional love, like the love she felt in her childhood. He held up his end of the bargain and, as if by magic, the chaos left their lives like a receding fog. Six months later, they returned to that same Italian villa for their wedding.

The benefits of living in synchrony with the currents of the cosmos are limitless. Immediately, the fruition of your plans will feel effortless and the objects of your attraction will spontaneously appear. It will feel as though you have literally caught some kind of wave, a wave of energy rippling out through the fabric of the creative field. You can assume a position of concordance with creative energy, or you can take on a posture of discord and antagonism. In order to foster wealth and success, it is imperative that you learn to live in sync with the currents of creation. But how, exactly, do you gauge whether or not you're swimming with the current or against it?

The Akranah lists a number of practical suggestions.

1) Meditate. If at all possible, allow yourself at least a half an hour every day to sit in silence and practice clearing your mind of thought. Allow your mind to generate a spontaneous image and then, as you breathe out, release that image to the universe. Allow a different image to appear, then breathe it out into the ether. Without mental static in the way, your body and spirit can become sensitive to the shifting currents of creativity flowing all around you.

2) Be open to instances of coincidence and synchronicity. The closer you approach the divine, the more you move with, rather than against, the rhythms and pulses of potentiality. Instances of coincidence and synchronicity are like signposts affirming that you are headed in the right direction. You will find such instances occurring more and more often as you progress.

3) Practice non-judgment. The more you are tempted to judge, the more you throw yourself out of sync. The need to judge is born of our frustration from swimming against the tide. Don't judge anyone for your circumstance, including yourself. Go an hour without judgment, then a day, then a week. Abstaining from judgment does not prevent necessary action. In fact, removing judgment is a

prerequisite to acting in sync with the world. As philosopher and martial arts pioneer Bruce Lee put it, "The moment we stop analyzing and let go, we can start really seeing, feeling—as one whole. There is no actor or one being acted upon but the action itself."

4) Be more aware of variances in the movement, or pace, of time. Like a canoe floating down a fast moving river and racing past the trees along the bank, when you move with the currents of the quantum field, you travel faster in relation to everything else or, put another way, the faster the rest of the universe moves in relation to you. This is experienced as time speeding up and explains why "time flies" when you are living life to its fullest.

5) Surround yourself with people you enjoy and admire, whose dreams mirror your own. When you are surrounded by people who are in sync with you and your intentions, they lend power to the gravitational force of those intentions, and you lend power to theirs. The infusion of synchronous energy goes far beyond mere emotional support. When you are surrounded by people who are moving with the currents of energy that buoy your intentions and propel them forward, they are, in effect, traveling with you, adding joy and power to your dreams.

THE SIXTH LESSON
The Law of the Central Figure

The Law of the Central Figure is the counterpart, and the counterbalance, of the Law of Ego.

The Law of Ego tells us to live in ecstasy, to step outside the confines of a more restricted self. After this is mastered, the Law of the Central Figure tells us to return to our physical selves with a new appreciation for the illusion of the singularity of consciousness. Yes, all the physical world is a stage. While you are here, joyfully participate as the star of the script of your life.

"All the world's a stage."
—*William Shakespeare*

"There are both kinds of heroes, some that choose to undertake the journey and some that don't."
—*Joseph Campbell*

WHAT WAS THE MOVIE *JAWS* ABOUT? WAS IT about a great white shark terrorizing a small bedroom community on the island of Amity, New York and the efforts of its police chief to stop the repeated attacks? Well, yes, this is the basic storyline of that movie. But it's *really* about Chief Brody and his quest to conquer his paralyzing fear of water. Water, in this instance, represents Brody's fear of his unconscious mind, his own primal nature, the ungovernable part of himself he refuses to acknowledge. The ocean represents Brody's animal aspect that desires to abandon the rules and bylaws of civilized life and, like the great white shark, consume the world's beauty—represented by the doomed swimmer Chrissie Watkins—whole.

What about the movie *Rocky*? Is this movie—which mirrors the story of The Epic of Gilgamesh, the greatest surviving work of Mesopotamian literature—about a small-time boxer given a once-in-a-lifetime opportunity to fight the heavyweight champ and his desire to still be standing after twelve rounds? Well, yes. That is the basic storyline of *Rocky*. But of course Rocky's true nemesis isn't Apollo Creed. It is Rocky's image of himself as a has-been loser, too tired and beaten down to manifest his dreams. Apollo Creed, in this instance, represents Rocky's own self-judgment, the part of himself convinced he'll remain an inveterate nobody.

Is *Star Wars* about the struggle between an evil galactic empire set on establishing a totalitarian regime and a resistance movement headed by a beautiful princess intent on destroying the empire's devastating new weapon, the Death Star? This accurately describes the dramatic twists and turns that make up the main plot of *Star Wars*. But at its core, the story is about Luke Skywalker, the young farm boy turned Jedi warrior who must make the central decision of his life—whether to dedicate his life to achieving power for the sake of doing good or to achieving power for its own sake. Darth Vader, in this case, represents Luke's suppressed temptation for ultimate power and his wish to become a machine free of the human torments of desire and loss.

The *Law of the Central Figure* tells us that you must understand how a mythic story functions before you can understand your own life story and your proper role in it. When you understand your life as a narrative that your intentions create, a narrative with you as the central character, you will learn not only how to take control of your future and attract wealth and happiness but also how to embrace your past as a necessary prologue to the incredible success that awaits you. You will learn that, by following the *Law of The Central Figure,* you can actually rewrite your past.

Imagine you were born rich, with a "silver spoon in your mouth." Growing up, you hadn't a care in the world, and a multimillion dollar trust fund awaited you on your eighteenth birthday. Imagine spending decades of your adult life bumbling through life, attending parties, blowing through relationships—

living like a teenager on a perpetual vacation. I have had several students and clients who, at one time in their lives, fit this description. And they were miserable. Every one of them felt lost and ill-defined, rudderless, and without any real sense of identity or pride.

After being introduced to the *Law of the Central Figure* and other lessons of the Akranah, however, their lives changed dramatically. One person used his millions to start a rehabilitation clinic in Florida for green sea turtles afflicted with cancerous tumors and other diseases and injuries. Another tapped into his connections with Hollywood luminaries and created a program that brings in film actors to conduct seminars for aspiring actors in the inner city. And another decided to pursue her dream as a filmmaker and, although she has yet to direct a full-length feature, is now producing music videos and commercials that have received international acclaim.

What fundamental change did these people make? They all made the conscious decision to cast themselves as the heroes, the *central figures*, of their own stories. Rather than being controlled by the shifting circumstances of their lives, they started taking action. Heroes are at their best when presented with barriers and obstacles. They pursue their goals with style and joie de vivre. They roll with the punches, celebrating each unexpected turn of events while not being subject to them. Like seasoned sailors, they adapt to changes in wind and current and weather, but they stay their course.

See yourself as the hero of your narrative. On a sheet of paper, describe yourself as a hero enmeshed in your own fabulous story, a central character who may have been tossed about by life, but who is about to grab the reins and take command. How, exactly, will this hero traverse the same spiritual threshold other bold men and women of history have stepped across to reach all the personal success and material wealth they knew they deserved?

What is your next move?

To bring the answer to this central question to light, you first need to better understand the structure of story.

Great stories are structured very much the way our lives are structured, in three distinct acts. But the best stories don't close down to a finite point. They open up. Their significance and influence continue to ring out like the sound from a bell, resonating beyond the events of the final scene.

Like great lives, great stories are, therefore, largely referential; the *spiritual* journey is the referent. Like the physical world itself, great stories are principally metaphorical of that higher frequency of existence—the divine, the realm of creation. For the protagonist, the hero of the story, moving through his adventure is like climbing a Himalayan mountain. The hero willingly puts himself into the field of danger to follow a plotted path to the summit. Once there, the truths from the story illuminate the entire sky and all the majestic peaks that surround him. From this vantage point, the hero is witness to the sublime.

In this sense, great stories are at once pedagogical and revelatory of the true nature of the divine and its relationship to our lives. By understanding the nature of story and the characteristics of the hero and the hero's journey, we can gauge our readiness to release our fear of overwhelming success and our willingness to access our own internal resources, to merge with the god within so that we may realize our most ambitious dreams—the dreams of a hero.

Do you want to know what it feels like to enjoy overwhelming success? Before you answer, ask yourself this: Does your current identity depend upon your resolute certainty that you are burdened with bad luck, that your efforts have little to no effect, and that it is your lot in life to play the perpetual sufferer, the person who never gets what she wants? Can you imagine any benefit to holding to this self-identity and this world view, such as safety or comfort? And are you ready to relinquish those benefits in exchange for the possibility of the world of surprise, the surreal experience of your dreams becoming real?

If I were to convince you that you could be safely and instantly transported to the moon so that you could walk its powdery surface in the comfort of a NASA space suit, you might think you wouldn't balk at the invitation. But then, when the reality sinks in that the airless surface of the moon can be hundreds of degrees hotter or colder than temperatures on Earth, you might think twice. We might use this fact, our recognition of the moon's treacherous and inhospitable landscape, to say no to the opportunity. In reality, it would not be the extreme temperatures holding us back. It would be the notion of surviving in an environment in which we had been told no human could possibly survive.

What strikes fear in us is the prospect of true uncertainty, of entering a world that is entirely different from the one we have come to understand and, to a limited extent, control. Breaking what appear to be boundaries to reach unlimited success can shake us to the core because we have been so very well trained to breathe the atmosphere of limitation. We've gotten good at it, and it's safe. Wading into a world of boundless success, on the other hand, is to enter a world without rule or reference—a whole new ball game. It's more than just walking on the moon in a heavy spacesuit; it's unzipping the suit, tossing your helmet into the powdery dust and sprinting to the top of the nearest lunar sand dune in the nude.

After more than two decades as a life coach and spiritual guide, I can tell you in all honesty that *most people do not want to be rich and famous.* Moving into a world of overwhelming success requires abandoning the familiar. And although the vast majority of us believe we desire extraordinary lives, the reality is that most of us are content—or, at least, content enough—with our lives exactly as they are and, unconsciously, take extraordinary steps to ensure that we maintain the status quo.

If you feel your life is characterized by failure and bad luck, then at least you can lay claim to this known, familiar commodity. Stepping out of the jail of failure requires squinting into the brilliant sunlight of infinite potential, which—as with a prisoner released from a dark cell into the light of freedom—can feel foreign, strange and more than a little dangerous. Forgive yourself for the difficulty you might experience during this transition. Take small steps around each obstacle, one at a time. Hold on to someone's arm. And trust that your eyes will acclimate and once again find their focus.

One of my clients is a ghostwriter who has made a very good living writing books for various Hollywood celebrities, sports stars and politicians. He is often approached by powerful people willing to pay him handsomely to write their dream book on political philosophy, nutrition, finance, travel, love, religion. When he asks them, "What do you passionately believe in?" more often than not these potential clients find themselves stymied by the question. Or they tell him they are passionate about their work and their families and so on but, nevertheless, exhibit no enthusiasm whatsoever. If passion were a magic wand of infinite power resting on a table a few feet away, these sleepwalkers would be unwilling, or unable, to walk across the room and pick it up.

Why? Because although they may be going through the motions toward success they are not yet fully committed to being the central characters of their own lives. In the worst case scenario, they have relegated themselves to living as a kind of secondary character: Disgruntled office worker. Frustrated mother. Aimless friend.

But there is a more hopeful possibility. If you wish to invite boundless possibility into your life, to emanate the glow of divine power everywhere you go, and you have taken definitive steps toward realizing your dreams only to see those efforts fail to unblock a rushing stream of effortless bounty, *then the problem very likely is that you are stuck in the first half of your story*, playing the role of the *reluctant* hero. You haven't reached what screenwriters call the "halfway point" of your script, the major turning point at which the hero stops running away from his demons, spins on his heel and runs straight toward that which he most fears.

In the movie *Jaws*, it's the moment that Chief Brody, his son in the hospital recovering from shock, decides to head out to sea with the colorful Captain Quint, venturing into the vast ocean he so desperately fears in a hunt for a massive great white shark.

In *Rocky*, it's the moment that Rocky Balboa lets go of his worst fear—being a man unworthy of respect—forgives Mickey for years of disdainful treatment, and runs down the stairs into the rainy street to hire him as his new manager.

In *Star Wars*, it's the moment that Luke Skywalker and the other passengers of the Millennium Falcon are caught by a tractor beam and pulled into the bowels of the Death Star where Darth Vader, the living symbol of his greatest fears, awaits.

Screenwriters call this "plot point" the "halfway point," or the "midpoint scene." Its significance rests in the fact that it represents the hero's greatest moment of trial and transformation, where the protagonist transforms himself from a reluctant, uncommitted hero to a hero of resolute action. But more than merely modifying his strategies, the hero must now dedicate his spirit fully to the enterprise of achieving his goal.

Many of us adopt a transformation of behavior without committing to a transformation of spirit. We elect to hold off the "midpoint scene" of our lives and remain stuck wandering the "first acts" of our lives' stories. Often, we let regrets over past "mistakes" keep us from transitioning into the next act of our story. It's as if Chief Brody were to say, "I can't go kill that shark now. I should have closed the beaches before the little Kitner boy was attacked! You know what? You guys go on without me." Or Rocky were to say, "I can't fight the champ! I've wasted so much time already. Let someone younger take him on!" Or Luke Skywalker were to say, "Let someone else fight the Empire. Here I was out looking for my lost droid while the aunt and uncle who raised me were back at the farm being slaughtered by stormtroopers. Sorry Obi Wan, but it looks like you're going to have to take care of that whole Empire thing yourself!"

None of these movie heroes became transfixed by the so-called "mistakes" of his past. Rather, each realized he was the central figure of his own story, and that a hero's story necessarily includes difficult, even desperate, times. In fact, this is the very sort of experience that catapults the protagonist into the heroic life. In the context of the hero's journey, a mistake is anything that prevents you from realizing the full arc of your experience. But setbacks, difficulties, even moments of utter despair, as seen from the perspective of the central figure fully aware of his role in the drama of his life, are crucial elements of the journey.

Everyone who has achieved something extraordinary in their lives can point to a great hardship that catapulted them into a unique trajectory that ultimately led to extraordinary achievement. Just as in great stories, our lives are punctuated by moments of extraordinary drama, events—sometimes wonderful, sometimes terrifying—that open doors to new relationships and new pathways of possibility.

As in any great story, the characters that come to populate our best-lived stories, our best-lived lives, are colorful people, fascinating, memorable and utterly unique, almost caricatures of themselves, infiltrating our dreams and pitching a tent inside our hearts. They are like great works of art, foreign artifacts from an exotic world. All these colorful people live fully from the core of their own self-definition, every moment fully and completely themselves, acting as the heroes of their own stories. And these people immediately recognize others who are also living from the center of their own self-definition.

If we can see each event as another thread in the tapestry of our lives, we can free ourselves from being tossed about like a cork in an ocean storm, elated by one event and dejected by the next. We can learn that the full tapestry of our choices through time, in all its color and glory, is our story, and behold that tapestry with gratitude knowing that pulling at one of its threads would unravel the entire cloth, leaving us with nothing. Celebrating the tapestry, even as you continue to weave it, leaves you with everything.

Once you cast yourself as the central figure of your own life, you can begin to create your own narrative in harmony with your own intrinsic nature, your own singular style, accepting the frustrations and obstacles of your past as integral to the plot of your life's narrative. Rather than regret what you may perceive to be mistakes of the past, you will marvel at how beautifully these events fit into the greatest story ever told—yours.

THE SEVENTH LESSON
The Law of the Dancing Demon

The Law of the Dancing Demon operates in cooperation with the Law of the Central Figure. It tells us that, as in any great story, the protagonist needs his antagonists, those who represent whatever it is the hero needs to overcome.

Our enemies demand the best of us, asking us to return to the central divinity that glows within us. Ultimately, our enemies allow us to test essential spiritual questions: Do goodness and compassion win out over ignorance and hatred? As eternal spiritual beings, are we willing to wager on love even when it seems as though the wager may not serve us? Our demons force us to answer these questions, reminding us what we believe in and, therefore, who we are.

"Your enemy is your greatest teacher."
—Buddhist saying

"Our enemies are our outward consciences."
—William Shakespeare

"It is the enemy who can truly teach us to practice the virtues of compassion and tolerance."
—Dalai Lama

THE *LAW OF THE DANCING DEMON* TELLS US to see our "enemies" for what they really are—manifestations of transformative energies in unappealing costumes evoked into our life experience by our own powers of attraction.

Our enemies can unnerve us, frustrate us and fill us with a sense of unease. At their most powerful, our antagonists can strike us with crippling blows; there is no denying this. The thoughtless actions of others can hurt us in ways that can change us permanently.

But our enemies need not leave us with less than we had before they arrived. Although our enemies most likely don't realize it, they arrive bearing gifts. Just as pollen sticks to the feet of a honeybee as it buzzes from flower to flower, inadvertently pollinating each one, negative people are unaware that they carry gifts intended for the rest of us. Even if they did know, they most likely wouldn't care. Still, opportunities for greater wisdom do, to continue the honeybee metaphor, stick to our enemies' feet. And when they come visiting your particular flower, you need only remember to collect them.

Our adversaries perform four essential functions: 1) They place barriers between us and the things we desire, which prod us to grow and evolve. 2) They provide opportunities for divinity, generosity and grace. 3) They expose the aspects of our being requiring attention. 4) They illuminate the borders of our spiritual landscape so we can better identify those energies with which we are most in sync.

Let me begin with the first point, how our enemies place barriers in our way and challenge us to move beyond them.

When I was a young girl growing up in Italy, my father, an inventor of specialized surgical instruments, and my mother, an actor and model, were often away on business, so I was often left alone in the care of my *tata* (Italian for "nanny"). My tata allowed me to watch one hour of television a day, and I talked her into letting me watch *Dallas* by convincing her it would help me with my American English skills.

If you've never seen the show, *Dallas* concerns the trials and tribulations of the Ewings, a wealthy Texas family of ranchers and oil barons. It starred Larry Hagman as J.R., the evil nemesis of the kindhearted brother Bobby, played by Patrick Duffy. At night as I went to sleep, I would imagine myself entering the world of *Dallas*, showing up one day unannounced to the Southfork Ranch and, just before the commercial break, introducing myself as the long-lost love child of Josh Ewing, patriarch of the Ewing family.

As soon as I imagined this scenario, I couldn't help but wonder, *Wouldn't it be better if J.R. were gone so that Josh and Bobby could run Ewing Oil without all the trouble and conflict? Wouldn't Bobby have a better life if his mean older brother, J.R., were to just disappear? Wouldn't I and the rest of the Ewing clan be happier if J.R. simply went away, never to return? Wouldn't it be better if we could make all our enemies simply go away?*

If we have decided to be the gods of our own personal universes, we have to take the question seriously, because we are no longer asking, *Why would God allow negative, hateful people to exist?* but rather *Why do I allow negative people to exist?*

Or, to bring it back to my little Dallas fantasy, *Why on earth should I keep J.R. around?*

We keep J.R. Ewing around because we need him! Bobby, J.R.'s benevolent brother, needs J.R. to challenge him and to bring spice and interest into his life story.

Who is Rocky Balboa without Apollo Creed? Or Chief Brody without the shark? Or Luke Skywalker without Darth Vader? Or Cain without Abel? Or Gilgamesh without Enkido?

We need our adversaries so that we may be provided barriers to overcome, obstacles that compel us to evolve and transform.

Even Yahweh of the Old Testament needs an adversary: Satan, with whom God enters a wager over the fidelity of God's most devoted servant. Satan's cynicism about human nature serves as a foil against God's certainty. In the ancient Hebrew, Satan literally means "adversary." In the New Testament, Jesus needs Judas to betray him so that he can carry out the mission of his sacred destiny.

The word "adversary" comes from the Latin word *vertere*, meaning "to turn." And so the first function of our adversaries is to require us to turn toward our inner divinity, to change, to grow and evolve. They are key players in the necessary trials of life who help us define not only who we are but also who we want to become.

Our adversaries teach us; they give us our homework. When we cannot complete the lesson on our own, we seek guidance from our other teachers, our spiritual guides. In this sense, our guides and adversaries work as a team to elevate our spirit to higher, more creative frequencies of being.

One of my first students was a litigator in a successful Los Angeles firm, on the fast track to becoming a full partner. Although he worked over twelve hours a day and often on weekends, he insisted he enjoyed the position. What he couldn't stand, he explained, was his boss, a senior partner whose personality so irritated my client that his increasing frustration was beginning to affect his marriage.

He and I discussed the lessons of the *Dancing Demon* at length. Before long, he came to realize his belief that he enjoyed his work as a tax litigator was, in reality, a rationalization. The fact was, it wasn't the work he enjoyed, but the salary and the prestige. Inside, however, he was dying.

The function of the young attorney's adversary, his boss, was to shed light on the chasm opening up in his unconscious mind, separating what he understood to be the ground of professional and family responsibilities from the ground of his own dreams and desires. The boss was like the single grain of sand in the oyster's shell, a mild but constant irritant that would ultimately lead to the production of something beautiful. In this case, my client came to the realization that he needed to change his life.

Soon thereafter he left his job at the big firm and went to work as an environmental lobbyist dedicated to protecting California's coast. He now loves his job and everyone he works with. And what does his wife think of all this change in his career? Not only does she "get her husband back," but his bravery to take a risk was all the incentive she needed to start her home-based business making pet toys from environmentally friendly materials.

Our enemies provide opportunities to love when giving love is the least obvious of all choices. The finest mushroom, the truffle, is one of the most difficult to find. The most legendary wines of Burgundy come from the most fickle of all grapes. And the most noble form of love waits like a precious jewel buried deep within ourselves, far beneath the rocky soil of hatred and judgment, just waiting to be unearthed. Every enemy carries in their hands a gift: the seed of opportunity for us to express divinity and grace.

Our adversaries can throw us into a state of spiritual upheaval, leaving us to ask, "Why do such people walk the earth?" But they also challenge us to use our imaginations, to question what we know about the physical or psychological pain they might be fighting on a daily basis. We can only imagine, and so we must do exactly that—*imagine*. Bear in mind that a jet flying 25,000 feet overhead always looks as though it is gliding gently through the air, even while—as the frightened passengers grip their armrests—extreme turbulence wildly tosses the plane about. Similarly, when the behaviors of your adversaries are most troubling, remember that their internal struggles are invisible to you.

Considering your adversary's internal struggles, as a primary impulse, does not require that you put yourself in danger or that you forgo your instinct to protect your own interests. Far from it. But by bypassing the conditioned fight-or-flight reflex, we can sometimes unearth hidden opportunities that others might well have missed.

Not long after my lawyer client decided to shift directions in his career, another client, who happened to be a lawyer for one of the largest talent agencies in Los Angeles, found himself in a similar predicament. He wasn't merely irritated by his boss, he absolutely loathed her. He was utterly convinced she had it in for him and would make his life a "living hell" until he quit. "She won't fire me. She wants to push me out," he told me. "If I quit, then she can spread the dirt that I collapsed under the pressure and I'll never find another job in this business."

So what key released him from his seemingly intractable predicament? In this case, my client really did love his job; it was obvious. He had wanted to be an entertainment attorney since college, and he didn't want to give it up. We talked about how one of the functions of the adversary is to make us initiate a serious introspection, to take inventory of those aspects of our character and our intentions that may be eliciting negative energies and behaviors from others.

Knowing he was a fan of the 1960s TV series, Star Trek, I posed this question: "Imagine that you are Captain Kirk, and you are placed in this situation. What do you suppose Gene Roddenberry [the show's head writer and producer] would have him do?" Half-jokingly, my client said, "It sounds kind of cheesy, but he always said the answer was love."

So that is what he chose. For the next thirty days he acted as though his boss were his favorite person in the world, a maternal figure wanting nothing more than to see him thrive. But it did not take a month for my client to see results. Within two weeks, his previously humorless boss completely transformed. As he put it, she was a different person. But something neither of us had expected came to pass in the coming months. She gave my client a promotion, which allowed him to work closely with her while representing the firm's top clients, a position that had never been given to someone so young. Now, as one of the highest-paid talent representatives in Los Angeles, his career is boldly going where it never could have gone before.

In this case, as with the other attorney's story, the adversary served as a catalyst for change. In other words, they were allowed to function properly as *adversaries* in the truest sense of the word: They forced each of my clients to *turn* in another direction. In the first case, the turn was outward in that the attorney elected to change his external reality, leaving one job for another. In the second case, the change was internal. When this client opened up to the possibility that the projection of his own energies was being reflected back to him, he began changing his outer world by instigating a change within himself.

Listen to this story of a Samurai warrior sent out to avenge an insult to his overlord. When the Samurai finds the man he has been sent to assassinate, he draws his sword and prepares to cut the man's head off. But just before he does the deed, the man spits in the Samurai's face. In reaction, the Samurai sheathes his sword and leaves. Why does he do this? He leaves because he refuses to kill in anger. By leaving the man alive, he exhibits a level of grace and divinity that the man finds devastating. Out of respect for the Samurai warrior, the man has no choice but to take his own life.

Of course, our intention is not to bring the witnesses of our displays of divinity to the brink of suicide. But we should expect such displays to be, in a sense, devastating. When the people around you are stuck operating from the lowest frequencies of their being, we must see this as an invitation to disrupt that arrangement. From Jesus Christ to Mahatma Gandhi to Nelson Mandela, great leaders do not reject the behavior of their adversaries. Rather, they use their adversaries as opportunities to display extraordinary grace and beauty. We can view the ignorant and mean-spirited person as an all-powerful enemy, or we can choose to see him as someone playing the role of adversary, someone inviting the rest of us to step into the role of wise and gentle teacher.

Now that I've described this concept in the abstract, let me give you a specific example.

In the documentary film *Prom Night in Mississippi*, the actor Morgan Freeman returns to his childhood home of Charleston, Mississippi to end a decades-long tradition of separate proms for blacks and whites by arranging, and personally funding, an integrated prom. While meeting with the high school administration, he is confronted by a man who, ostensibly, has concerns about security for the prom. But with his hostile tone and folded arms, this angry man lets everyone know he is not only challenging the idea of an integrated prom but also confronting this Hollywood big shot, personally, for rocking the boat in his quiet Mississippi town.

How do you suppose Morgan Freeman responds to this "good ol' boy" staring him down from across the table? Does he stand up with fists raised, ready for a fight? Does he use his formidable intellect to embarrass the man in front of his friends and colleagues? No. Instead, he agrees with him, saying that, yes indeed, security is important, adding only that security personnel should abstain from wearing firearms (as this could send the wrong message).

And in that instant of divinity—call it "a totalitarianism of grace"—everything changed. Assured that he had been heard, the angry man leaned back and the muscles of his face completely relaxed. The rest of the people at the meeting nodded to one another as witnesses to a kind of miracle. The man had allowed the bigotry that he still carried inside him to bubble up to the surface like puss from a boil. And rather than condemn the man, Morgan Freeman treated him like a patient with a suppurating wound, someone seeking the gentle touch of a healer.

One of the heroes of this story is, of course, the man who unwittingly revealed his antiquated racist views. It was as if he had been nursing a malignancy deep within his psyche and had now coughed it up into the bright sunlight, where it could die. In a sense, that man honored Morgan Freeman by allowing him, the very symbol of his past contempt, to surgically remove this decades-old tumor of bigotry using the gentle instruments of grace and forgiveness. This was, of course, the inevitable product of Mr. Freeman's intention.

Once a client of mine called me from his home in Palm Beach in a panic to tell me that, upon arriving home one afternoon, he discovered a developer and his two-man crew bulldozing a section of his back yard in which he had been constructing a small Zen sanctuary.

The sanctuary was ruined. He wanted to call the police. He wanted to call his lawyer. He wanted to run down the hill and beat the man unconscious with a tire iron.

After we talked, he decided to view the developer as a demon bearing gifts. And what he ultimately did was stunning. He grabbed three beers from his refrigerator and walked down to where the men were working. He approached the developer and said, in the calmest voice he could muster, "I don't know if you realize it or not, but you fellows are bulldozing my yard. I figured that rather than having a big fight about it, we could all have a beer and talk this over."

As it turned out, the developer was fully aware that he was bulldozing my client's property. But, as he explained it, he thought it was "all good" because he planned on replacing the damaged landscaping once he was finished.

Was the developer in the wrong? I would say so. But the point is, it doesn't matter who was right. Had my client called the police, the police would have told him that such civil matters over the destruction of property are issues to be brought to an attorney. Had he called his attorney, the lawyer would have explained that lawsuits are expensive and that, even if he were to win the suit, he would still wind up losing money. He would have advised my client to somehow make peace with the disrespectful developer.

The sanctuary was destroyed. Blaming the developer wouldn't bring it back. But forgiving him— demonstrating the art of divinity—might.

My client's indigenous plantings had been bulldozed into the dirt, but what rose out of that raw soil was an opportunity to rise into divinity, to act as a god on earth, which is exactly what my client did. The developer—who almost certainly had done this sort of thing dozens of times before—was prepared for the usual battle over land rights. After all, the most that could happen to him would be a judge ordering him to replace the landscaping. What he wasn't prepared for was the landowner approaching him at this higher frequency, displaying divinity and, by example, inviting others to do the same.

The developer replaced the landscaping as promised. And my client, certified in transcendental meditation, taught him how to meditate. His new friend then offered to repave my client's lengthy driveway for the cost of materials, a promise he kept, saving my client tens of thousands of dollars. To this day, they still surf together and fill up on fish tacos every Thursday at their favorite oceanside restaurant.

Your adversaries illuminate the aspects of your being most in need of your attention.

A good friend of mine was recently telling me about an author she admired. His books and CDs had helped her through a painful divorce and the loss of a close friend to cancer. However, one thing had been bothering her: "He mentions his eight kids on one page," she said in a huff, "and then a few pages later talks about the problems of overpopulation! I mean, how hypocritical can you get!?!"

The first thing I suggested to her was that, until she were given the opportunity to ask this author to explain the apparent disconnect between his professed beliefs and his behavior, she would be better off withholding judgment. (Even then, judgment wouldn't serve her, as I'll discuss in the next chapter.) The next thing I said to her was, "It sounds like hypocrisy really gets your goat." "Yes," she said. "It really drives me crazy!" "And how many instances of hypocrisy do you think you witness in an average day? One? Five?" She jumped in, saying, "Five? Are you kidding? Hundreds! Thousands! Don't you read the papers?!? The politicians, the news pundits, the celebrities—it's practically a national pastime." "Right," I said. "So if hypocrisy upsets you, you'll either need to lock yourself in a basement somewhere or learn not to be so upset by instances of hypocrisy. That or prepare to be upset for the rest of your life."

Here is a story about a farmer who could never refuse to engage any instance of hypocrisy he encountered, told to me by my spiritual teacher, Sri Swami Katananda.

Once, a farmer in a small Indian village was walking a cart full of hay down a narrow dirt road. The exceptionally rich and nutritious hay was for his family's cows that, due to a recent drought, were thin and ailing. But before long, he happened upon someone else's cow sleeping in the middle of the road, directly in his path.

It so happened that, within the boundaries of the village, it was against the law to allow one's cows to sleep on the roadways.

The humble farmer had never thought much of the law. "Cows sleep where they will!" he often complained. "Everybody knows that." When he recognized that the cow in the road was, in fact, owned by the very politician who had passed the ridiculous decree, he decided to challenge this hypocrisy. He refused to simply walk around the animal.

After several attempts, the farmer found that he could not prod the cow from its comfortable spot in the warm dust.

As a last resort, the farmer took some of the expensive hay from his cart and held it under the cow's nose. The cow raised itself from the ground and followed the farmer to the side of the road, where it happily munched the hay, allowing the farmer to pass freely.

But then, after walking only a short distance further, the farmer found a second cow sleeping in the road, which he recognized as yet another from the politician's herd. And rather than simply walking around it, he took more hay from his cart and lured it to the side of the road.

And then he came upon a third cow, and lured it to the side. And then another. And another. Soon, the farmer realized that he had used up half of the hay he had intended for his own cows back home.

The farmer was faced with a decision. He could either spend what was left of his precious hay luring cows off the road or stop engaging these symbols of the lawmaker's hypocrisy.

After careful consideration, he decided to save his hay for what mattered most, his own family's cows.

He chose to walk around.

Like the farmer, we must choose whether or not to dedicate our time and energy to engaging every instance of hypocrisy—and every other wrong that confronts us—or to save those precious spiritual resources for the things that matter most.

There is no shortage of things in need of improvement, no shortage of hypocrisy, or injustice or thoughtless cruelty. And so we must pause before laying even a small piece of ourselves at the altar of "principle." The wiser strategy, the story teaches us, is to be more discriminating, and to dedicate our talents and energies to those causes upon which we can expect to exact some measure of real influence. You cannot fight every battle, because your cart can only hold so much hay.

So many things in the world can drive us mad if we let them. For environmentalists, it's the witnessing of nature being destroyed. For the politically minded, it could be instances of corruption. To the humanitarian, it might be the continuing problems of poverty and hunger.

There is no denying the fact that some people are intent on bringing sadness and negativity into the world. But we must remember that our adversaries serve to remind us that, though we can attract what we want into our own lives, we cannot control everything. Sadly, there will be less nature tomorrow than there is today. There will be instances of injustice tomorrow, just as there are today. And, as Jesus Christ suggested some two thousand years ago, there will always be poverty and hunger. To think that any one of us could wipe out any one of these problems is to indulge in vanity. We can, however, bring more divinity and grace to the aspects of our consciousness most vulnerable to hurt and frustration and, as Mahatma Gandhi suggested, "become the change we want to see." It's not so much about "saving the world" as it is about saving *your* world.

Our adversaries help us to illuminate our spiritual plane, allowing us to more precisely map the topography of our own spiritual landscapes. They help bring into stark contrast whose frequencies most resonate with our own, and whose energies most interfere with our own. When we wander into a field of dissonant energies we, in effect, sever our communication with the universe, enveloping ourselves within a cloud of disruptive static.

Earlier, in the lesson on the *Law of Synchrony*, I discussed the importance of surrounding yourself with people whose energies resonate in sync with your own. As a spiritual coach for over a decade, I have found that the importance of placing yourself in the company of like-minded, like-spirited people is often underestimated. Sometimes, in the spirit of self-reliance and independence, we can talk ourselves into believing that, as long as our intention is strong enough, we can shield ourselves from the affects of the asynchronous energies of others. Our sense of duty often leads us to elect to shoulder the burden of toxic relationships or continue to work in a hostile environment because we have convinced ourselves that we can, by sheer willpower, shake off any negative influence.

In reality, being in sync with the people around you is a prerequisite to allowing your powers of attraction to summon and solidify the manifestations of your desires from the dynamic field of creation. It is so crucial, in fact, that when students tell me they have completely lost their bearings, that they can't follow their bliss because they have completely lost sight of what their bliss might be, I advise them to forgo thinking long-term for a while and think only in terms of the people they spend their time with. If your energies, your beliefs, your ambitions and your aesthetics are discordant from those of your colleagues, friends and loved ones, then this discord can prevent you from tuning into the flow of cosmic energy. Like an airplane flying through a lightning storm somewhere over the Pacific, the static interference makes it impossible to get your bearings so that you can find your way safely home.

The only way out of the storm is to surround yourself with people whose energies resonate with your own.

So how do we identify those people whose energies most perfectly harmonize with our own? If the people in your life fill you with hope, energy, confidence and serenity, then you are most likely already running with the right herd. If, however, you are still uncertain, then once again *you can turn to your adversaries for assistance.*

There is one particular form of adversary whose influence, if unrecognized and unchecked, can prove particularly nefarious: the vampire. The vampire is the enemy you willingly invite into your life as a friend. The vampire establishes intimacy only so that he or she may siphon the nourishment of your energy, your talents, your relationships, your finances or your body, someone who has practiced and perfected, often over the course of a lifetime, the art of manipulation.

The fail-safe test for recognizing a vampire has nothing to do with garlic or holy water or holding up a mirror. Simply ask yourself this: *Is this friend of mine dedicated to delivering as much love and protection and support and generative energy into my life as I am dedicated to delivering those things into his? Is he at least bringing as much joy into my life as he is presently able or, rather, does this relationship feel like a one-way street in which I am the only one who gives?*

Like any other adversary, the vampire invites you to revise your life, to examine your priorities and to identify those belief structures that have fallen into disrepair. The vampire forces you to reassess, and invest in, your personal value, as well as the value of your time and energy. Once you recognize that you are being used, you can ask yourself, *How has my self-image become so withered that I would allow myself to be used so? And what will I now do to restore that image to its former glory?*

Of course, if you ask yourself these questions and determine that, in whatever relationship, you are the one giving far less than you are receiving, then it might be a good time to fetch that mirror, after all.

If a relationship feels like a one-way road, you have most likely already trespassed into the territory of the vampire. But like any other adversary, the vampire, if allowed to act in his proper role, can redirect you to the shoulder of that road to warn you that you are heading into oncoming traffic.

View vampires and all other adversaries as "wrong way" sign posts on the road of life. Think of them as light houses warning your ship away from the treacherous rocky shore. If you find yourself confronted with more and more adversaries every day, take this as a sign that (remembering the root of the word "adversary") you need to *turn* your boat in a completely new direction.

Even if, at the surface level, your life appears to have all the things that "should" make you happy—a big house, a prestigious position and all the other accoutrements of success—if you continue to discover more and more adversaries appearing in your way, take this as a signal that it may be time to shift directions in a decisive manner. It might be time to consider a new career, possibly moving to another part of the country, or even reexamining your primary relationships.

Hatred for our enemies is no more than the outward projection of our own frustration over our failure to achieve bliss, reminding us to redouble our efforts; the splinter in our enemy's eye reminds us to remove the beam from our own. Rather than indulging in hatred for our adversaries, we are well served to remember how each may very well present an opportunity for growth and, often, greater prosperity.

At the very least, our adversaries act as warning buoys, helping us to steer ourselves away from negative, polluting energies that such people represent. But they can do so much more for us. Think of the high school bully's victim who becomes the martial arts superstar; the abusive boss that impels the employee to start his own successful business; the millionaire celebrity agent who learned self-respect after standing up to a bigoted drill sergeant.

Though it doesn't happen often, sometimes our adversaries return to us later in life, not with hostility and anger but with sincere regret, begging us, hat in hand, for our forgiveness. Should we offer our forgiveness, remembering the crucial, ultimately positive role they may have played in our lives?

The Akranah offers an interesting perspective. According to *The Law of the Dancing Demon*, the concept of forgiveness is nonsensical. Forgiveness is necessarily predicated on the fact that the person asking for forgiveness is materially different from the person who committed the original offense. They have learned; they are wiser; they are repentant; they would not commit the same offense again.

Therefore, according to the *Law of the Dancing Demon*, the malefactor no longer exists. In a sense, the offending person has sent an emissary, an improved version of himself, into the future to solicit forgiveness *on the sender's behalf*. In the ancient language of the Akranah, the word for forgiveness suggested that the mistreated person recognized this new person as distinct from the old. Pronounced *hah nah zool*, it meant, literally, "He (she, it) is not born (of the living)." Put another way, *That person doesn't exist any more*. *Hah nah zool*, then, had a far more comprehensive function than the modern concept of forgiveness. The offender, operating from ego-consciousness, is diminished to the level of a kind of dead husk whose usefulness has passed, a shell he needed to cast off in order to emerge in the form of materialized divine consciousness.

The repentant divine self asking forgiveness, then, is very much like a butterfly asking to be forgiven for the ugliness of its abandoned cocoon.

Hah nah zool: I see that you are not the cocoon; I see you as the person who has emerged from within. It, the cocoon, is not part of the living world, and I now recognize that it never really was.

The function of our adversaries is to spin us into an entirely new trajectory, down a new path leading to greater wealth and abundance than anything we envisioned for ourselves before they entered our lives.

THE EIGHTH LESSON
The Law of Non-Attachment

The Law of Non-Attachment is related to the Law of the Central Figure. As you write your life's story, you must trust the universal creative force to inspire you, to signal you to alter your course when necessary. Staying open to these navigational signs requires a certain degree of surrender and trust, a willingness to step into the field of the unknown, where everything is possible.

When we wrap our arms too tightly around the anticipated results of our intentions, we make it difficult for our dreams to breathe. Use your mind to create powerful intentions, but then allow these intentions to interact with the intelligence of the universe, where they will be refined and magnified.

"When the violin can forgive the past, it starts singing. When the violin can stop worrying about the future, you will become such a drunk laughing nuisance that God will lean down and start combing you into his hair."

—Hafiz, Sufi Poet

"When you are free of attachment, you are like a paper lantern unperturbed by the wind."

—Buddhist saying

THE *LAW OF NON-ATTACHMENT* ADVISES US TO maintain a certain objective disconnection from the events in our lives, a degree of distance from the transient ups and downs of the vicissitudes of circumstance. The *Law of Non-Attachment* reminds us that we are infinite beings of boundless possibility and power, and we would do well to expand the view of physical existence by incorporating the perspective of our immortal, spiritual selves. To operate within the highest realm of creation means we are no longer limited by our own minds and can access the spirit of universal intelligence—that infinite organizing power that surrounds us all. But to accomplish this, we must be willing to relinquish the comforting illusion of control.

May I tell you the story of the Taoist farmer who loses his favorite horse? His neighbors exclaim, "What bad luck!" The farmer says, "We'll see." Then the horse returns, followed by an entire herd of horses. "What good luck!" the neighbors say. "We'll see," says the farmer. The farmer's son then breaks his leg training one of the horses. "What bad luck!" "We'll see," the farmer says. Finally, delegates of a local warlord visit the farmer to recruit his son to fight in a war based on a personal vendetta against a rival warlord. When they see that the son is in no condition to fight, they excuse him from duty. When the delegates leave, the neighbors say, "Now that really is good luck." To which the farmer replies, "We'll see."

The point of this story—which, as I'll explain later, relates as much to the *Law of the Central Figure* as it does to the *Law of Non-Attachment*—is to show how fruitless it is to judge the goodness or badness of any individual event until we have had the benefit of understanding the event's place in the context of the complete narrative of our lives. All the farmer knows, at the last point in the story, is that losing a horse led to his son being allowed to stay at the farm rather than going off to an ill-conceived war. He abstains from judging during the ups and downs of his life because he doesn't yet know what role these events will play in the whole of his story.

How would most of us feel if we were that farmer and had just lost our cherished horse? We would likely feel devastated, either because our livelihood depended on the animal or because we loved the horse as a beloved member of the family, or both. And how do most of us feel when we look back on such emotionally difficult events? We regret them. We grieve. We replay the events in our heads over and over trying to figure out how we might have prevented the tragedy in the first place. We view the event through the pinhole of the present. And with that small snapshot, it is so very easy to paint a gloomy picture of the rest of our lives that we often fail to see these events and their ramifications in the context of the full narrative, as necessary scenes in the epic tale of our own spiritual journeys.

Rather than viewing the present through the wide aperture of eternity, we perceive our entire lives by peering through a keyhole.

Once you step outside your present circumstance long enough to see yourself as the main character in a gripping saga, you will allow yourself to walk through each scene of your life with a carefree perspective, celebrating the inevitable vicissitudes of life with a sense of adventure, with trust and faith—and a healthy sense of detachment.

We are sometimes unwilling to simply enjoy the view of the setting sun; we must capture it on video. We cannot enjoy the rain on our skin; we must comment upon it, offering witticisms about the joys of walking in the rain. Once, a Buddhist student and his mentor walked around a bend in the mountains and were confronted by an amazing view. "How lovely, that mountain in the sunlight," commented the student. "Yes," said his master. "But what a pity to say so."

Our desire to frame each moment for our uses —to lock down the meaning of something, to press a moment into the locket of memory so we can reminisce later, or to use the moment to make judgments about all the potential consequences of that event—can prevent us from experiencing the moment as it is.

What is the meaning of life? What is the meaning of a flower? What is the meaning of a bee landing on the flower and settling on the petal and then lifting itself into the perfumed air? What is the meaning of you witnessing these things and feeling joy at the sight of them?

Penetrating each moment in an attempt to quarry every experience for its utility is like dissecting a hummingbird to claim ownership of its beating heart. You can have the dead heart, or you can enjoy the knowledge that inside the hummingbird hovering outside your window sits a tiny fist of muscle beating a thousand times a minute to drive its delicate and powerful wings. But you cannot have both.

Why are we so compelled to control rather than simply experience? Fear, mostly. Fear of our own weaknesses, our perceived inability to fight through adversity. We are like downhill skiers who cannot concentrate on the next turn because we are too busy worrying about the possibility of crashing and breaking a leg.

But what would mountain skiing be without the joy of gathering momentum on a vertiginous downward slope? Or the long stop-and-go ride up the mountain and the laughter of conversation as you dangle a hundred feet above the ground on the ski lift?

The ups and downs of life are a wonderful and necessary part of the ride. Why judge them in the midst of the experience? The time for examination is later, in calm reflection, when we can gather whatever lessons the experience has to offer.

While heading to the slopes, our job is simply to pick out a stylish outfit and wait for the lift to take us up. As you head up the mountain of your life, remember to ski with people whose company you enjoy. When you wipe out into a snowbank, really wipe out, then laugh as both your skis slide down the mountain on their own. Ski with joy and fearlessness until the sun goes down. You bought the lift ticket. Get your money's worth and make certain that, in the lodge, with your feet up enjoying a drink with your friends around a roaring fire, when it comes your turn to talk about your day, you've got a good story to tell.

One of the greatest poems of the last half century was written by the American poet James Wright. "A Blessing" centers on a simple moment: the author and one of his best friends, poet Robert Bly, visiting a couple of horses munching grass in a field in rural Minnesota.

The last lines of the poem go like this: "I would like to hold the slenderer one in my arms,/ For she has walked over to me/ And nuzzled my left hand./ She is black and white,/ Her mane falls wild on her forehead,/ And the light breeze moves me to caress her long ear/ That is delicate as the skin over a girl's wrist./ Suddenly I realize/ That if I stepped out of my body I would break/ Into blossom."

The word for "stepping out of [your] body" is *ecstasy*, meaning, from the Greek, "outside of where you are standing," or "to step outside yourself." For most of us, it is only in the midst of extraordinarily moving moments, surrounded by loved ones and the beauty of nature, that we allow ourselves to experience this feeling of stepping outside ourselves long enough to "break into blossom." We've all had this feeling of losing ourselves for a moment, that sensation of elevating into the highest frequency of being where your identity commingles with the domain of infinite wonder and possibility, the sensation of falling into God.

Think of the last time you had one of these experiences, when you really surrendered yourself to the moment. Were you concerned about the future, or your job, or some ongoing argument with your boss, or next month's mortgage payment, or what time it was, or anything else? Did you interrupt your moment of revery and awe to say to yourself, *Now this is truly a special moment. I should really try to make this last!* Perhaps you did have such a thought, the very kind of concern that takes you out of the moment. Often, when we dare to unmoor ourselves from our attachments and allow the currents of cosmic energy to pull us toward an experience with the divine, we sense danger and we panic. We resist. We grab for the safety lines of attachment. We fear. We judge, and we thus anchor ourselves to our judgments. Rather than living in the moment, we assess and reassess everything around us, becoming more and more attached to our beliefs and all the attendant subjects of those beliefs.

And what does attachment do? It disrupts the communication between our physical and spiritual selves. Attachment short circuits our ability to enjoy either the ephemeral *or* the eternal. The more we become attached to specific outcomes, the more judgmental we become about ourselves and others. And the more we indulge in judgment, the more attached we become to specific outcomes.

Writer Deepak Chopra has written extensively about his love for the game of golf, suggesting that it is one of the most spiritual games ever invented. If you've ever watched a professional golf tournament, you may have noticed how, once they've reached the top of the leaderboard, even seasoned pros often fall apart during the last few holes, hitting terrible shots and missing tap-in putts that, under ordinary circumstances, they could make wearing a blindfold. The annals of golf history are littered with heartbreaking stories of men and women cracking under the pressure of a possible victory, their hopes shipwrecked along the rocky shoals of *attachment*.

Equally well-known among golf fans is the axiom that once a PGA golf pro wins his or her first tournament, winning the second and third comes to that player relatively easily. Why would this be? Because of the nature of attachment. When a golf pro considers the prospect of winning his first tournament, he or she imagines a life-changing event, after which nothing will ever be the same again. *Once I make that last dramatic putt on the eighteenth green with all the cameras flashing and the gallery cheering, everything will be different*, they tell themselves. *Self-doubt will be a thing of the past! People will love me as never before! My kids will look up to me! My friends will respect me! I will have finally made it!*

Of course, not long after the golfer hoists the golden trophy, a fine patina begins to form over its surface. He soon discovers that the initial thrill of victory is transitory; it will not sustain him, or his sense of self-identity, indefinitely. The spoils of success, much like the symbols of mythology, resist our attempts to capture them, to lock them in a frozen posture like a big game hunter mounting his latest kill.

In the chapter on the *Law of the Dancing Symbol*, I discussed how the symbols of mythology must be allowed a certain freedom of movement in order to remain translucent and open. This way, the symbol can act in its highest capacity, as a passageway to the divine. Similarly, you must allow the gleaming trophies of your success—the house, the car, the business or the trophy itself—to dull a little as time goes on, as they are meant to.

The trophies of our success have but one function: to open up new avenues of experience. The function of a plane ticket—or for that matter the plane itself—is to provide the experience of flying, and whatever experience awaits you at your destination. The function of a Nobel Prize is to allow you more access to influential scientists, so that you too may increase your level of influence. The function of a wonderful meal at an exclusive restaurant is so that you can share the meal, and good conversation, with a friend or lover. The function of a garden shovel is to provide the experience of gardening, of plucking the fragrant tomatoes from their vines and, ultimately, of serving a wonderful meal to friends.

Placing a stranglehold on the trophies of your success is like spending your nights polishing your prize watering can, turning it into an extension of your identity and, therefore, into a kind of fetish, an idol— all while your neglected plants wilt of thirst. In the same way that the symbols of myth must be allowed to change and "dance" so that we may pass through them to the divine, the trophies of success, be they houses or cars or businesses or awards, must be allowed a certain freedom of movement to best serve us, so that we may pass through into a world of greater possibility.

Win the trophies of success, then pass through them into the next set of experiences in which more trophies will be collected. Pass through these into the next new set of experiences, and so on.

My student, the Olympic medalist in swimming, put it best. After studying the Law of Non-Attachment for months, she said to me, "I realized that it wasn't so much my love of beating other people that drove me to winning so many races. It was my love of swimming, the sensation of my body moving fast and efficiently through the water. And then it occurred to me, if I were to go for an ocean swim with all my medals around my neck, I'd drown."

Golf professionals typically find a first victory to be elusive. The reason these pros often find it relatively easy to achieve their *second* victory is that they have learned to place the trophy—and all that follows—into the proper perspective. That is not to say, however, that these objects of victory are illusory; nor are they just monuments to vanity. Of course, they are more than this. Or, at least, they *can be* more than this. Only when the victor yokes her identity to these objects, only when she pulls them tight to her chest and hoards them like a mother centipede wrapped around her clutch of eggs are they trivialized. The tragedy of the dragon of Western mythology is that it hoards its cache of gold, and the princess whom it has taken prisoner, for the sake of ownership and control and attachment. Then, even the beauty of its possessions become lost to it until it is enraptured by the attachment, a prisoner attached to attachment itself, a pitiable creature dizzy with paranoia and greed breathing fire at anything that comes near.

Imagine visiting the home of an aging athlete hoarding his many awards—so many dusty symbols of his athletic prowess locked away in a trophy room. Imagine this person hoisting up each golden statue, bragging about his past, recounting each victory and trying to regale you with his many conquests—the famous people he has met, the women he has dated, the competition he has dominated.

Should we admire him, or should we pity him for his attachment to his long forgotten conquests? As much as society tells us to admire such a person, we cannot help but recognize something slightly unattractive about the spellbinding attachment to symbols of accomplishment. There is a difference between celebrating one's accomplishments and becoming attached to them. The first involves a choice to *share*, to live in ecstasy, to leap out of the confines of physical identity and into a larger world. The other is inward in its character, like a great hawk granted the most splendid wings in the animal kingdom deciding, for its maiden voyage, to fly into itself.

In the classic movie *Sunset Boulevard*, a struggling young writer, played by William Holden, becomes involved with an aging Hollywood star so attached to her past accomplishments that she becomes a kind of wandering ghoul, a spider sitting at the center of the web of her own ego, a web which ultimately ensnares and kills the young writer. The writer, in turn, is attached to the fading star's money, to her power, to the doors of opportunity he hopes she will open for him. Both characters are so driven by their attachments that they fail to truly connect with the people around them, and their stories end in disaster.

How sad, these stories of those who choose to cling to their accomplishments, or to their past "mistakes," or to the objects of their wealth, or to the objects of their poverty. They are sad because such attachments shut us off from all the possibilities that swarm around us every moment, all the other experiences and friendships and all the things we think of when we consider what it means to feel *alive*.

If a bird were to become infatuated with its wings, it would remain in the nest, pluming its feathers, neglecting the feeding of its young. Narcissus became so attached to his own image that he stared at his reflection in the pool until he died.

How, then, can we gauge whether or not we have grown too attached to the fruits of our past and future efforts? How do we know when we have crossed the line that separates healthy celebration and healthy pride from destructive attachment? Are we to stop caring whether or not our hard work leads to anything of substance? Or, to put it in the terms of my friend and student, a PGA golf pro, "Shouldn't I care whether or not I win the tournament and the millions of dollars that come with a first-place victory?"

The answer is, *Of course you should care!* But once you have established for yourself what you have identified as your goal, you must—like a sailor who has set his sails and rudder—lean back a bit and enjoy the salt air, the sound of the gulls jockeying about the mast and the gentle loll of the ocean waves.

Yes, *care*. But care as someone whose identity does not depend on the next win. Care with love, and compassion, and humor and grace. Care from the perspective of the being you truly are—infinite and boundless and divine. As your god-consciousness choreographs the events unfolding around you, have faith that you know exactly why you chose to play things out this way. Whether you win or do not win a particular battle—a golf tournament or a business deal or anything else—try to maintain faith that your inner divine self is operating from a larger map, a long-term strategy of which you may not be completely aware.

When I asked my client, the PGA tour pro, about his most cherished victory, he made no mention of any trophy or multi-million dollar prize, or even his precipitous rise to fame. He spoke nostalgically of a perfect shot he'd made during a most improbable tournament win—a 5 iron into a left-to-right wind over a pond onto a postage stamp green—and the moment he felt the ball compress against the club face, then relinquish its mass to the seduction of an upward trajectory and lift soundlessly into the late afternoon sky. At that moment, he said, the prospect of winning or losing fell away. Past and future dissolved and only the present remained. Even the distinction between himself and the club, the ball, the crowd, the salty afternoon air—all of it simply disappeared.

"In that moment," he said, "all I could feel were the dimples in the ball. I had this image that each dimple was a tiny foot, that they were my feet. And with each rotation of the ball, my feet were digging in and climbing a little higher into the air."

He told me that when he indulges in being attached to the outcome of every shot, his score determines his attitude. Without attachment—when he revels in the sunshine and the birds and the fact that he plays golf for a living—his attitude determines his score. That's when he wins.

The world is rife with such overwhelming experiences of divinity, aglow with the light of glorious beauty. But in order to step into that beauty, we first must remove the chains of attachment. By maintaining our attachments—to objects, to events, to outcomes, to regrets and all the ephemera of material experience— we make it impossible to enter the invisible highways of consciousness that lead back to our higher selves, to the majestic cathedral of cosmic potentiality.

When we relinquish attachment, we open ourselves up to all the conduits of energy available for exploration and elect to be more receptive to the small coincidences and moments of synchronicity pointing the way to other pathways. In that moment of letting go, the manifold portals of divinity become visible all around us.

Attachment to the Energy of Others

In The Bhagavad-Gita, Lord Krishna explains to his disciple, Arjuna, the nature of attachment: "When a man finds delight within himself and feels inner joy and pure contentment within himself, there is nothing more to be done. He has no stake here in deeds done or undone, nor does his purpose depend on other creatures. Always perform with detachment any action you must do; performing action with detachment, one achieves supreme good."

Notice first that Krishna doesn't say, "One *will* achieve supreme good." He says, "One *achieves* supreme good." This suggests that once you are immersed in the performance of the act, without dependence, or even reference, to the fruits of your efforts, *you are already in the midst of achieving supreme good*. Also take note of the words "supreme good." Winning a prize or landing a job or defeating an enemy in battle are all laudable goals, of course, but they are incidental in comparison to the "supreme" act of tapping into the divinity of the moment, transcending time and space and connecting with the energetic flows of cosmic creation.

Also notice that Krishna says, "nor does his purpose depend on other creatures." This is important, and worthy of further discussion.

Think of the moodiest person you know. Have you identified them? Can you see his or her face?

There's a good chance that you just thought of someone who has some element of control over your life—a boss, a close friend, a parent, or a son or daughter. Perhaps it is your life partner. The point is, the person you thought of is likely someone whose moods affect you directly, someone whose energy directly affects yours. This is why you are keenly aware of every fluctuation in their sense of happiness and peace, because, like the rising and falling water supporting every boat in an ocean harbor, his or her energy shifts conduct themselves into the energies of your own life.

Imagine walking over a footbridge made entirely of bamboo and rope spanning a thousand-foot deep river gorge. Scary, right? Now imagine doing the same thing while some daredevil teenager walks the same bridge fifty feet in front of you. He's a real troublemaker, this one, and so he decides to swing the rope bridge back and forth with all his might, jumping up and down and laughing hysterically as he shakes the lines to the point of breaking because, even with all his recklessness, he's convinced the ropes will hold.

When we yoke ourselves to the emotions and behaviors of emotionally turbulent people, it is very much like following that teenager over the rope footbridge. Their instability becomes our instability; their chaos, our chaos.

It's important to keep in mind that there is no such thing as dabbling in chaos. If you choose to traffic in chaos, even a little—say, to maintain a relationship with just one chaotic personality—you invite into your life all the chaos in the universe. Like opening your front door just a crack to experience the winds of a category five hurricane outside, you entice the storm of chaos to rip your door from its hinges and inundate your life with its rain.

Those whose emotions go up and down like a roller coaster are what I call "emotional day traders." Like day traders on Wall Street, emotional day traders gauge their happiness and self-worth in reference to superficial objects and phenomena. My stocks are up, and therefore I'm a smart, successful person. My stocks are down, and so I'm an unworthy failure.

When we link our happiness or sense of self-worth to the whims of emotional day traders, we block ourselves from the infinitely expansive creative source that sits like a placid reservoir at the still core of our spirits. Rather than simply being enthralled by *our own* personal attachments, we become enthralled, vicariously, to those of another person over whom we have little control. Before we know it (as I discussed in the chapter on the *Law of Synchrony*) our energy frequencies match the frenetic, shifting frequencies of the other person.

Cross the rope bridge of life alone. Or better still, follow a guide whose confident, calm and surefooted steps actually stabilize the bridge and keep it from swaying.

So how does all this relate to the above conversation between Krishna and Arjuna, and what lessons are we to gather up and take with us?

While taking surefooted steps to fulfill your desires, you must not attach yourself to the fruits of your efforts. Resist linking your happiness to those who, because of their ungoverned attachments, behave like emotional day traders, their sense of well-being ticking up or down with each new event. Put yourself in league with people who have successfully mastered the art of non-attachment. When you follow people with this sort of confident stride—smooth, steady and surefooted—you can actually feel their presence stabilize the many bridges we must cross in our daily lives. Trust the grin of the Taoist farmer who says, "We'll see," the one who refuses to lay claim to every event as it appears. Allow every event and each new circumstance to wash over you, to come and go as softly as a butterfly resting on the back of your hand. As you walk across life's bridges, try to resist inspecting every piece of rope, the integrity of every knot, and judging every step you take.

Make a daily practice of trusting the events unfolding before you, and their proper place in the universe of your experience. The bridges of life are not composed of bamboo, or knotted ropes, or steel or anything else susceptible to the corrosive powers of time. We are suspended by a robust latticework of trust and faith interwoven. Enjoy the view, knowing fully that the bridge will hold you.

THE NINTH LESSON
The Law of God

The Law of God is at once a divine invitation and a call to action. The most wonderful thing about harnessing the ability to effortlessly manifest your desires is that you are blessed with limitless opportunities to share with others. Once you choose to harness the invisible currents of bounty that surround you, your dreams begin to flow into your life, one after another after another. Soon, the objects of affluence become mere baubles, diversions, as simple to replace as they are to acquire. The burden of being a god is that your identity, as you previously understood it, disappears. As a god on earth, you choose to participate in the physical world primarily so that you may give.

"He who drinks from my mouth shall be as I am, and I shall be he."

—Jesus Christ, from The Thomas Gospel

"Single is the race, single
Of men and gods;
From a single mother we both draw breath.
But a difference of power in everything
Keeps us apart."

—Pindar, the sixth century B.C.E.

OF ALL THE CONCEPTS ADDRESSED IN THE Akranah, the *Law of God* is by far the most challenging. The *Law of God* describes how, as you move up the channels of energy into higher and higher frequencies of spiritual consciousness, all manner of duality dissolves away to the point that your desires and the manifestations of those desires fuse into a single quantum event of spontaneous creation.

Those are the very words my master spiritual guide used to introduce me to the *Law of God*. As you can see, it is difficult to capture the essence of the *Law of God* with words, precisely because of the nature of the law: Words exist in a world of duality, and serve largely to describe dualities—this versus that, this happened before that, it is or it isn't raining outside, and so on. But these tools of communication, born of a world of duality to describe the physical world of duality, disintegrate as they approach the subject of the *Law of God*, the matrix of boundless love and creation in which duality, like a two-dimensional object in a three-dimensional world, has no place.

And so the Kakranah, the protectors and teachers of the wisdom of Akrah, have for centuries retold the story you are about to read, a story retold only to the highest level of aspirants in the ultimate stage of their education. To begin to understand the underlying meaning of this story, you will need to open up to the more creative parts of your consciousness, the artist inside you. Don't think prose; think poetry. For a few moments, let go of concrete definitions, and think in terms of metaphor. Try to resist the temptation to try to wrench linear, denotative meaning out of the story. Rather, allow the story's connotative energy to probe your mind and spirit. Too often, we follow our past training that tells us to mine a story for meaning with the aggression of a gold prospector blowing up the side of a hill. There is no need to dismantle the mountain to mine its riches. Walk to the top of it. Relax. Wait for the sunset. And allow your mind to reach a deeper sense of joy and gratitude as you take in the view.

An Elephant Made of Mice

One day in a great forest, an elephant found himself facing a tiny gray mouse standing in the middle of the path. The elephant, acting out of fear born of the stories he'd heard of mice crawling up elephants' trunks, said defensively, "You're so ugly, I just might eat you!"

Ordinarily, this threat would frighten any sensible mouse away. But this particular mouse, who just so happened to be a god, said, "Please do. You look so very hungry."

Confused and angry, the elephant summarily swallowed up the mouse. Convinced this was the end of the matter, he carried on with his day, eating leaves, rolling in mud, and—emboldened by his victory over the mouse—stomping up great clouds of dust to terrify other mice who, after witnessing their friend being consumed, quickly scampered into the shadows of the underbrush.

That evening, the elephant fell fast asleep. In the middle of the night, he was awakened by a strange itching sensation in his ear. Suddenly, from that same ear, the mouse appeared.

"Sleeping well?" the mouse asked the elephant, who was now cringing in terror. "I've had a dreadful time getting to sleep. Would you care to know why?"

The elephant, shaking with fright, nodded his head.

"You see, I first went into your stomach, where I found all sorts of wonderful things to eat, and so I helped myself to a lovely dinner. Still, I was hungry. So I went to your heart and considered eating that as well. But at the last second I decided against it. And I'm glad I did because, when I ran up into your head, I had a lovely time swimming through your dreams, and I saw that they were the dreams of someone destined to become a god."

"Me? A god? No, no! I could never be a god! I'm barely an elephant!" said the elephant. "You, a mere mouse, can pass in and out of my body at will. You have complete power over me!"

"So if you were a god," said the mouse, "and you had power over me, would you simply crush me underfoot?"

"Of course not!" exclaimed the elephant. "God is love. I suppose that, were I truly a god, I would house you inside me, and feed you, and give you water, and offer those very same accommodations to all the other mice along my path."

"Would you indeed? Then why not act as though you are a god, and see what happens?" suggested the mouse.

And so, following the mouse's advice, the elephant spent the next three years doing exactly that. Every mouse the elephant happened upon was kindly invited to live inside the elephant's body until, in no time at all, his stomach was full of mice, as well as his legs, and his head, and his trunk, and every last compartment of his massive body, until there was no elephant body left at all, only mice.

The elephant's body had become a living monument of the elephant's ceaseless love, a manifestation of compassion. He was no longer a mere elephant, but rather an elephant-shaped creature, an elephant made of mice whose skin rippled with the frenetic energy of a million grateful inhabitants, the very animals that to him once represented nothing but animosity and fear.

Then, late one night, when the dreams of all the tiny mice danced together like a million blades of grass swaying in a breeze, the elephant realized a perfect dream he could never adequately articulate—a dream so expansive that no one mind could ever contain it. He saw the world not through his own eyes, but through the thousands of eyes that travelled throughout his body, as well as through the eyes of every mouse in the entire forest.

He awoke into a different world. And because he awoke into a different world, he gave himself a new name. And his name was "The Elephant Made of Mice," a proper name for a god on earth.

The next day, The Elephant Made of Mice went about his usual business, until he happened upon yet another mouse on his path. Only this time, because he could see through this mouse's eyes as well as his own, he recognized immediately that standing before him was no ordinary mouse. He was confronted by a mouse-shaped god.

The mouse's name was "The Mouse Made of Elephants."

The tiny creature looked up at the massive pulsating silhouette standing before him and said, with a glitter in his eye, "You're so beautiful, I just might eat you!" The Elephant Made of Mice winked at the little god and replied, "Please do. You look so very hungry."

Within this seemingly simple story, all the seven key concepts of the *Law of God* are visited. The key concepts are 1) Ego and the teleologic error 2) The disintegration of duality 3) The function of fear 4) The concept of circle time 5) The non-linearity of love 6) The nature of gratitude 7) Giving and the *Law of Attraction.*

Each point is essential, so let's examine these key concepts one by one, beginning with ego and the teleologic error.

The Teleologic Error

Which is more intelligent, a human being or a whale? Of course, we know what human beings are capable of. But humpback whales are known to locate deep undersea rivers and use these conduits to broadcast their songs thousand of miles around the world. And not just any songs, but ancient songs passed down from generation to generation, songs whose syntax and meaning remain a mystery even to the scientists who spend their lives studying them.

What about the human versus the honey bee? Bees live in fantastically complex societies that cooperate in the gathering of pollen, the building of nests and the raising and feeding of their young. They navigate vast distances guided by the Earth's magnetic currents. And through the language of dance, they communicate to other bees the exact location of the best flowers, including the types of each flower and how much food is available.

How long would it take any one of us to learn to feed, and play, and communicate if, one morning, we were to find ourselves in the body of a whale? If you were to wake up in a bees' nest, in the body of a bee, how long do you suppose it would take you to catch on and get with the program? A couple of hours? A day? A week? They are just bees, after all.

We human beings are quick to consider ourselves superior to any other creature we meet. But this reaction springs from a flawed supposition. Philosophers and scientists call it the "teleologic error." It refers specifically to the misguided notion that human beings are the "endgame" product of evolution, the centerpiece of all creation, the singularly unique creature around which everything else revolves.

This error is, as you might suspect, the product of ego and arrogance. Not so long ago, the human ego clung to the reassuring notion that the sun revolved around the Earth—that is, until this was definitively proved to be false. The ego nestled into the comforting idea that, because the sun and the moon and other celestial objects seem to move at a constant pace, time must be, in reality, consistent. Then Einstein showed time to be in a state of constant flux and variability. And for centuries, each dominant world religion insisted that their particular prophet—Jesus, Buddha, Mohammed—spoke only to the most elite members of their religion. But now, more and more people study the teachings of all the world's great prophets under a much more ecumenical light, and receive them as sources of inspiration and wisdom.

In the beginning of the elephant story, the elephant makes the classic teleologic error. Because he is physically larger than the mouse, he sees the mouse with revulsion, suspicion and disdain. He thinks himself superior and fails to consider the possibility that he has just crossed paths with a bona fide god.

The lesson is this: Forget the notion of superior versus inferior. Every creature, every spirit, has its place in the continuum of energy and information; the tree frog basking on the branch is no more or less important to the life of the jungle than the mighty jaguar stalking the path below. The dragonfly no more dreams of being an eagle than the kidney dreams of being the heart. Every object and every living being represents the light of the divine projected through the prism of the quantum field upon the canvas of the physical plane. Each is a necessary brush stroke of paint in a masterpiece composition.

Our instincts tell us the death of a blue whale represents a greater loss than the death of, say, one of the millions of krill that whale has fed upon. And in the scheme of the material universe, this can seem to make perfect sense; compared to the tiny krill, the rare blue whale represents a pinnacle achievement in the orchestration of information and energy into a massive system of complexity and order. But the moment the whale dies and its body sinks to the bottom of the sea, its flesh is seized upon by hagfish, and lobster, and bristleworms, and prawns, and isopods and every manner of scavenger who depends upon the periodic boon of what biologists call a "whale fall."

And now the whale's vast body of complexity —its beauty, its participation in the symphony of energy that makes up the physical world—is once again taken in by nature, which is insatiable for beauty, and so refuses to let any of that beauty, any life, go to waste.

The separateness of things is illusory, the appearance of individuation no more than a practicality, a way for us, as the individuated particles of God consciousness, to more fully interact with all creation. Our souls are cast out into the world of separateness, where we work and plan and love and feel and allow ourselves to fall for the whole charade, and then we return to celebrate all that we have experienced.

All is referential. We are all, therefore, participants in a spiritual metaphor.

When sunlight passes through a diamond, it casts upon the wall a shifting geometry of greens and blues and reds and yellows and every color in between. Ask yourself, *Which color among them is superior to the rest?* Which is the best? Which one shall we keep? Obviously, such contests are folly.

God is the sunlight. God is everything we experience. And like every other object and phenomenon in the universe, we are one of the separated frequencies of that light—God's light individuated. And the diamond, the quantum field, is the sphere of existence where we interact with the divine.

Of all the colors cast out by a diamond, which one do you most object to? None, of course. Every color the diamond projects is divine. To diminish one color is to diminish the beauty of the sunlight that contained it. In the same vein—though the behavior of some can, at times, cloud this deeper realization—all creatures are the beautiful manifestations of God.

The Disintegration of Duality

Imagine two tornadoes forming out of a powerful Texas storm, each twisting down to the ground, snapping electric wires and uprooting massive trees as if they were delicate tufts of grass.

You might see the tornadoes as separate phenomena. But to the meteorologist, they are but two aspects of a single, larger weather system, the natural and predictable outgrowths of the chaotic churning in the clouds above. The meteorologist sees, veiled inside the carnival of muddy air ripping through the most destructive tornadoes, vortices spontaneously forming inside the rotating mass, appearing and fading out and appearing again.

We see a funnel cloud. The meteorologist sees an entire weather system, miles wide and thousands of feet deep, a system they've been tracking for days.

The more the meteorologist knows, the more he cannot help but see the interrelated, inseparable nature of his world. Similarly, the more you understand the true nature of reality, the more the apparent separateness of things reveals itself to be an artifact of the limits of our own perception. We see ourselves as separate from the objects of the physical world—as well as separate from each other—only because it is pragmatic to do so. Like the two gods addressing one another at the end of the elephant story, we must cultivate our ability to see past this surface projection to the divine light that is the projection's source.

The Function of Fear

In the lesson on the *Law of the Central Figure*, I used the movie *Jaws* to elucidate the necessity of our obstacles and objects of fear in the overarching narratives of our lives.

There is an old story attributed to the indigenous people of the Amazon, presumed to have come from the Yanomamö tribe. In this story, called "The Story of the Painted Parrot," a gray parrot is terrified of birds with colorful wings. One morning, he sees a bright red bird and attacks it, but the red bird flies off. Then he sees a blue bird and attacks that bird as well, and it too flies away. Then a green bird, then a yellow bird, and so on. At the end of the day, the gray parrot discovers that the colors of the birds have rubbed off on him, his feathers now adorned with all their brilliant hues.

Another gray parrot approaches the painted parrot and asks him, "May I fly with you? I am terrified of birds with colorful wings. But I can see from your wings that you are afraid of nothing."

When we reach the end of the story of "The Elephant Made of Mice," the elephant has learned to see the objects of his fear not as something to run from, but something to elect to interact with, as doorways that can open to his higher, more powerful self. Ultimately, the tiny mouse-shaped god finds himself joking with his fellow god about the benefits of facing the objects of our fears so that we may subsume their power.

Our fears are not weaknesses. Like the "impurities" of bronze metal, the fears we carry, once we have successfully incorporated them into our consciousness, serve to make our spirits more pliable, more capable of bending in the strong winds of adversity. Dare to acknowledge your fears as the flexible and resilient palm tree acknowledges the wind, as a force of nature whose power is real, *but limited*. Trust that, in the early hours of the morning, the air will be calm again, and you will still be standing.

The Concept of Circle Time

"It's a poor sort of memory that only works backwards."
—Lewis Carroll, from *Through the Looking Glass*

The word *Boddisatva* comes from the Sanskrit words for "being" and "illuminated." According to world mythology author Joseph Campbell, one of the more salient features of the Boddisatva's illuminated character is in the way that he "realized his identity with eternity and at the same time his participation in time."

So what does it mean to realize your identity with eternity and at the same time your participation in time?

Before we look into this question, let's take a moment to look at time. According to leading physicists such as Stephen Hawking and Brian Greene, although we experience time as a constantly forward-moving phenomenon, the forward arrow of time has no more mathematical validation than does a backward arrow of time. Put another way, *there is no reason that time should move forward; it is only our experience of events that moves forward.* Viewed objectively, time has no forward motion except that which our perceptions impart to it. Much like film moving through a projector, the frames of time are shown in forward sequence only so that the movie can make sense to us; this is how we experience the world. Every film you ever watched was wrapped around the film canister long before you bought your ticket.

Is this an argument against choice, against free will? After all, taken to the extreme, this would be an argument for "scientific determinism," the view that all the subatomic particles of the entire universe—like so many tiny billiard balls—were set in motion long ago, and their trajectories can no longer be altered. Scientific determinism is a stone's throw from fatalism, which argues not only that free will is illusory, but that the end of the story—our story—is not a happy one.

But here's where scientific determinism breaks down: Subatomic particles refuse to follow the same physical rules that govern the motion of billiard balls. These particles hover in a cloud of potentiality, awaiting an outside influence—the influence of observation or of consciousness—to lock them down to one single quantum state. The subatomic cauldron is a fluid and dynamic soup of infinite possibility where particles interact with other particles across vast distances instantaneously, bypassing the limits of the speed of light. Given what physicists have learned of quantum space, the appearance of the cause-and-effect linearity of time must be replaced by another model, that of "quantum," or "circular," time.

This understanding directs us to replace the concept of fate with that of destiny. Fate is set in stone.

Destiny, on the other hand, refers to a world that is dynamic and fluid and directly responsive to our consciousness and intention. The higher up you move through the frequencies of being the more you approach the quantum realm, and the more you experience time as circular in nature rather than linear. In that realm where the divine and the mundane interact, time draws into itself until, ultimately, the individual frames of experience are projected simultaneously, like a roll of movie film played out in an instant. The closer you move toward the divine, the faster time seems to move. This is why "time flies when you're having fun."

One of the most extraordinary implications of the non-linearity of time is that your intentions can attract events that manifest *in the past*. Inversely, it tells you that particularly powerful intentions you have yet to create—but are destined to formulate—may have already crossed over ahead of you to sow the seeds of your desires.

The elephant story begins very much as it ends, drawing in upon itself to circumscribe its events within a full narrative circle. When the mouse admits his temptation to eat the elephant, we know that the elephant, or at least his physical identity, has already been entirely consumed, and supplanted, by the higher identity of godhood.

This idea of circle time might strike you as puzzling at first. Consider the following scenario. Say, for example, you were planning to be away for the holidays on business, but the trip was cancelled. If you desire with passionate emotional intention that your son or daughter visit for the holiday, you might discover that—for reasons they cannot explain—it had occurred to them to buy a plane ticket at a discounted price a full month ago, long before you knew you would be staying home. As counterintuitive as it may seem, the more you lay claim to your own inner divinity, the more you will be able to manifest events in the future *as well as in the past*, in effect influencing your universe *retroactively*.

The Non-linearity of Love

If you understand the concept of circle time, then you are well on your way to understanding The Non-linearity of Love.

Many people acknowledge that when you begin to love someone or something your love radiates outward, from that time forward, into the universe, ultimately to be experienced by others. But more than this, love radiates out in the frequency of the divine, carrying with it the unmistakable signature of God. Therefore, love is not bound by our own limiting perceptions of the linear arrow of time.

Have you ever had the experience of someone unseen reaching out to you, supporting you through one of those times in your life that felt like an endlessly long, cold night, a voice warming your spirit enough to allow you to survive those dark hours until, finally, you could perceive a promise of hope like the onset of the morning sun?

Who was this presence, and from what place, what time, were they sending their protective warmth? Was it God? Was it a spirit of someone long departed, calling out to you from the past? Or was it someone in the present, reaching out from another part of the world, or a kind spirit from another realm of existence?

As a child, you may have felt the presence of some angelic figure guiding you through these darkest of times, periods of great confusion and dismay. The non-linearity of love suggests that the someone reaching out very well might have been looking at a picture of you a hundred years in the future and thinking, *I hope that sad looking little girl in the photo knows how lovely she is. I wish I could reach out and let her know.*

With that thought, they are sending—they *will be* sending—love to you, to your place and time, and into your life. Love is the highest of all energies, subject to none of the mundane rules of time and space. Whenever a person's consciousness emits love, the effects are holistic and immediate, its sphere of influence without boundary.

In the elephant story, we are to understand that the love between the elephant and the mouse is not fated, but it *is* destined. The moment they extend love to one another, their relationship is no longer subject to the governance of linear time, nor are they vulnerable to the erosion the passage of time brings. Not only is any act of love permanent and omnipresent, but it has always been so.

The Nature of Gratitude

Although the elephant story does not suggest it explicitly, there is a hidden message concerning the importance of gratitude. As we create powerful images of the things we desire, it is crucial that we feel an equally powerful emotion of gratitude for those things *before* we have received them in order to guarantee our desires manifest themselves in our lives.

It is essential, also, that we include gratitude for the approaching opportunities to leverage our prosperity and influence to enrich the lives of those around us.

In the story, when the elephant insists he could never be a god, the mouse recommends to the elephant that he act as though he were a god and "see what happens." It suggests a considerable leap of faith on the part of the elephant, to put his comfortable modalities of fear and cynicism aside long enough to invite his own incipient divinity to appear.

I will admit that, when my greatest spiritual teacher first explained to me that the elephant's willingness to act as a god in hopes of someday becoming divine refers to the highest forms of gratitude, I failed to see how these two seemingly disparate concepts—that of faith and that of gratitude—were, as he suggested, explicitly conjoined.

As he explained to me, the connection is this: True gratitude is something felt *before* a gift is given, not *after*. *Responsive*, or *reactive*, gratitude—something felt and expressed *after* the event one is grateful for—is inherently provisional. This lower form of gratitude is given only in return for, and subsequent to, the reception of the gift. True, *proactive* gratitude, however, is an expression of love, which, as I discussed earlier, is not contained by, or subject to, the linear, forward-directed arrow of time. Proactive gratitude is a function of faith, faith in the loving, unbroken relationship between you and your inner divinity, between your material self and the cosmic eternal in which your divinity constantly participates.

Just as love, in its purest and highest form, transcends duality—beyond cause and effect, cause and consequence—instantaneously filling every region of space and time, the same can be said of gratitude, but only when one feels gratitude daily, regardless of the nature of the day's events. When gratitude is given only reactively, under the parsimonious, contractual *quid pro quo* agreement, gratitude as payment for a good deed or blessing, we undermine the ageless and boundless nature of gratitude and, by extension, of love.

Both love and gratitude should not be given only in return for other things, or you risk diminishing both to the level of banal commodity. If love and gratitude are provisional, something only to be given in response to, and in consideration for, something else, then you are not truly giving either. At best, you are giving a counterfeit token in place of the bona fide article—the energy of God's love and magnificence, *your* love and magnificence bounded by no contractual arrangements or, for that matter, limits of any kind.

Giving and the *Law of Attraction*

In the elephant story, the elephant learns that generosity and sacrifice (from the Latin *sacer*, meaning "holy," and *facere*, meaning "to make" or "to do") is a prerequisite to achieving divine bliss.

Hundreds of books have discussed the concept of attraction, many of them wonderfully describing the powerful relationship between consciousness and the manifestation of physical phenomena. But most fail to explore the crucial relationship between attraction and giving. Over the years as a master of mind potentiality, I have found that many of my more advanced students find the usual discussion wanting, questions left unanswered.

"They tell you how you can attract a big oceanfront property and fancy cars," one such student remarked to me recently, "but they don't tell you what the point is! So that's the great secret to the meaning of life, the acquisition of property? The ups and downs of commerce?"

To answer such earnest and probing questions, I find it useful to refer to whatever literature the student is already familiar with. In this case, the student was a producer in Hollywood, and so—as I did in the chapter on the *Law of the Central Figure*—I used a familiar movie to serve as the landscape for our exploration of this important question.

With his groundbreaking, Oscar-nominated movie *Avatar*, the brilliant James Cameron once again redefined the art of cinema. The movie tells the story of the Navi, the indigenous people of a lush, idyllic moon, called Pandora. When an energy company and their army show up to displace, or destroy, the Navi in order to mine the "unobtanium" sitting beneath the Navi's sacred village, sparks fly. In the end, the Navi, with the help of a lovestruck, paraplegic Marine in the avatar of a Navi's body, defeat the evil corporation, sending them and their powerful army packing.

The movie leaves little doubt that we are to "read" the energy corporation as the bad guys. They are careless, violent, proudly exploitive and motivated purely by profit. The Navi, we are to understand, are different. They refuse to exploit nature for their own immediate uses and, in contrast to their invaders, choose to live in perfect synergy with their environment, operating on a higher frequency of existence, connected with their luminous, divine force, Eywa.

But are the Navi so different from their corporate antagonists? In the fictional world of Pandora, nature seems to exist exclusively to serve the needs of the Navi. Plants dutifully illuminate the Navi's path as they step upon them. Horses and flying dragons wait in designated areas for the Navi to arrive and leap upon their backs for yet another joy ride. No need to spend any time getting to know these animals or bring them any food in exchange for their services. No need to train them, either. Conveniently, they are all plug-and-play; simply connect your hair to the animal's tail and direct it, with your thoughts, anywhere you want to go. Even Eywa, the Navi deity, seems to exist solely for the Navi's benefit, storing Navi memories and offering useful advice to help the Navi continue their idyllic way of life.

What's missing here? In a word, *sharing*. Not sharing in the sense of "I'd like to share a story with you," but real sharing, as in, "Let me share my meal with you." What's missing is sacrifice. What the soulless mining company and the Navi have in common is that they both see the outer world strictly in terms of personal use, reducing the wonder of all creation to the banality of its mechanical utility.

I should point out that *Avatar* is a visually stunning movie and James Cameron—in addition to being a stalwart champion of the environment—is one of the great writer/directors in the history of moviemaking. And given that he is a six-foot-two male born in 1954, it's perfectly understandable that, given all his good fortune, his imagination would generate a virtual world that hews closely to his experience, a world seemingly created for his pleasure and entertainment.

Add to this the fact that, like the rest of us who grew up in the West, Cameron was raised under a self-centered interpretation of Genesis 1:27-28. If you accept the King James translation, we are to hold "dominion over the fish of the sea and over the birds of the air and over every living thing that moves upon the earth." However, when you learn that other translations of the original Hebrew replace the word "dominion" with "responsibility" or "care" or, to use the Hawaiian word, *kuliana*, you see that this verse, like so many in the Bible and other great religious texts, is in fact another dancing symbol, not a monolith truth frozen in ice, but a vast gallery of understanding, a grand museum of manifold interpretations to be entered by way of any one of its many doors.

Why so much focus on this one, final concept in the lessons of the *Akranah*? Because this lesson is by far the most difficult, as well as the most important.

The noble honor of sacrifice is the final piece of the puzzle, the keystone to tapping into the ground of all creation, spontaneously and effortlessly manifesting your desires and traveling through life as a living god.

What is the most recognized symbol on the planet? It is the crucifix. Now consider this question: What single word best characterized Christ's death on the cross? The answer, of course, is *sacrifice*. Finally, ask yourself what immediately followed Jesus' sacrifice. What followed was *paradise*, the reunion with God.

The more you sacrifice for others, the more you awaken your divine powers, your inner god. Consider this: From one perspective, you might view Jesus Christ as a reluctant participant in the ancient ritual of scapegoating, symbolically representing the unlucky receptacle of an entire tribe's accumulated sins, banished to die of hunger and thirst in the vast open desert.

From another perspective, Jesus is not only a willing participant in his own slaughter, but indeed the main choreographer of the horrific drama of his own torture and death. From this perspective, his prediction during the Last Supper that one of his apostles would betray him is viewed as an instruction, as in, "So that I may sacrifice myself as planned, can one of you please betray me?" To make his intentions of sacrifice more clear, Jesus likens the dinner's wine to his blood, the bread to his flesh. Only the most noble among his disciples, Judas, understands the message—the encoded instruction—and is moved to step forward to facilitate Jesus' plan, to assume the difficult role of turncoat so that his spiritual master and friend might consummate his mission on Earth, the mission Jesus was born to carry out.

Viewed from this perspective, Judas becomes a saint. Jesus offers up his own "flesh and blood" to feed his followers, and then reenacts this same ritual, giving up his flesh and blood upon the cross. Immediately thereafter, he ascends to paradise to once again commune with the divine.

A sense of your own divinity allows you to sacrifice without fear. After sacrifice comes a full reunion with that divinity—the bliss of paradise.

How could Jesus have communicated this message more clearly?

When you delight in the opportunities for sacrifice, you designate yourself as someone operating not from your local identity, but from your universal self, defining yourself not as a single drop of water, or even as a single river, but as the vast sea of divinity to which all water returns. Once you do this, all the previously blocked channels of energy finally open up to you so that all your desires can flow toward you as frictionlessly as water rushing down a winding mountain stream.

From that point forward, you will *choose* to participate in the world of duality, the world of time and individuality and judgment, but your smile will bely your secret. You will know. And other gods on earth will see your smile; they'll sense that you realize how the conscious participation in the costume ball of life is a choice, and that participating fully, with awareness of both the eternal and ephemeral aspects of your being, transforms the day's business from a chore to a celebration. You will be welcomed into the elite circle of the gods. You will be recognized for your wisdom, solicited for your guidance, and presented opportunities to help others achieve their dreams. Align these manifested dreams that you helped others achieve like the steps of a staircase. With each step, you will ascend further into the glow of the infinite creative field, the source of your limitless power, the birthplace of your divinity.

As a god, you will witness the world as the majesty of your own personal creation, an extension of your own joyful spirit with which you *choose*, daily, to interact. Your physical manifestation is the vehicle through which you have chosen, for a time, to experience yourself, to celebrate your wonder while giving gratitude for the blessing of living in a world of your own spontaneous creation.

In your life as a god, everything and everyone is enjoined in the glorious service of everything and everyone else. You attract wealth and affluence, and it is good. You share the wealth and abundance with others, and it is good. You influence others to attract endlessly bountiful wealth into their own lives, and it is good. And they, in turn, attract more affluence and bounty into your life and into the lives of those around them, and it is good.

Say the words, "Let my desires be brought to my feet. Let there be bounty and wisdom and love and sharing. Let me create a stream of opportunities to sacrifice for the sake of others and receive the bliss of limitless power that follows true giving."

Let there be love. Let there be the bounteous manifestations of my intention, so that I may share those blessings.

Let there be light.

Choose to trade envy for celebration of another's happiness. Trade accumulation and hoarding for flow and generosity. Trade animosity and fear for acceptance and infinite flexibility.

To be a god on earth is to be a walking paradox, an invisible presence participating in the physical world of dualities for the express purpose of allowing divinity—unity, creativity, unbounded power and love —to express itself. Your divinity is like the wind that fills the sails of an ancient ship carrying precious treasure, wind passing through the chambers of cosmic instruments to create the celestial music of all creation.

When you fail to make sacrifice and love the guiding polestars of your being, your ship lolls in the doldrums, and the music stops. But when you remember that your ship is filled with food for the hungry, the winds stir up again.

When love and sacrifice serve as your guiding forces and your intention is focused on generosity, you find yourself dancing on the deck as the captain of your own chosen vessel, its cargo stuffed to capacity with everything you desire, a ship heading up a beautiful river that winds through a strange and luminous fog into the wide open sea. Soon, an island will come into focus, and upon your landing, a stranger will approach you on the beach and take you in his arms.

It will feel like a reunion, because that is exactly what it will be; you have met this person before. This person is your divine self, who has long ago lost any sense of time, or separateness, or ego.

And in that embrace, your physical and divine selves will become an entity united, ready once again to embark upon yet another journey into that strange and ephemeral world of dualities, ready to put on a different mask and step back into the great hall of the material world, where the dance of celebration goes on.

And how should you behave, as a god on earth? As you glance over to the person next to you on the airplane, ask how you might offer him or her some small kindness—a shoulder to cry on, a person to listen to their troubles. What might you offer the frail old man struggling to lift his luggage from the conveyer belt, or the frightened animal at the local rescue shelter that longs to be held and loved, or your own child, or your mother, or your partner who can drive you so crazy, but who dearly needs to hear how they are appreciated and loved?

What on earth is a god to do?

The answer is clear: Act as a god. This is what you are, a god in human clothing, another silly god grinning and singing and dancing down the streets of the cities of her own invention, looking for another chance to offer the gift of selfless love, manifesting dreams and giving them away like candy at a parade.

The moment you commit yourself to truly living as a god, everything in your life will begin to change. You will become so empowered to effortlessly manifest your every desire that you will ask yourself if you are dreaming. And are you? Of course you are! Only now you have woken up inside your dream and taken control of where your dream goes next.

Read and reread each lesson in this book until you feel you fully understand it. Every day, commit to living out just one of the lessons of the Akranah. Feel the changes in your consciousness, in your heart and in your soul. Every day you practice these lessons, you will feel more powerful. You will feel your dreams align themselves before you like dutiful soldiers awaiting your next command.

And every day, you will more fully realize that it was never powerlessness that you feared. Powerlessness can become an object of comfort, a fetish. What frightens us is the prospect of becoming all powerful, our dreams becoming real. We fear that once our dreams are realized, we will no longer have anything to hope for.

You will always have dreams. There will always be another experience, and therefore another experience to be shared.

Like a child who tries to hold his breath and discovers that he need not breathe at all, or who flaps her arms pretending to fly and feels her feet leaving the ground, it's entirely natural that—in the first seconds of any new reality—we feel a twinge of real anxiety. But directly following this feeling of terror comes a feeling of exhilaration, and possibility, and delight.

Ask yourself, *If my dreams did start manifesting spontaneously, would I be ready to face the consequences? How would my life change? And do I welcome those changes?*

If you practice each of these lessons daily, prepare for your dreams to become realized.

The first days of living like a god will feel surreal, as if you have just woken up in the middle of the night in a strange bed. The bedroom looks familiar, but somehow transformed. You notice a faint glow of light peeking out from beneath a closet door. You open the door and discover a stone stairway twisting down into the earth. You walk down the stairway and emerge into the dawn light, where you see a beautiful woman in flowing white robes pointing at something, directing your attention. You look up to see a massive wooden ship waiting on a wide channel that flows to a protected bay. Behind the bay, nothing but open ocean.

You have seen this ship before. You are already familiar with every corner, every cabin, every plank of wood. The busy members of the crew halt their preparations and look down at you, some smiling in recognition, motioning for you to head up the gangplank.

As you ascend the plank, you see someone standing at the top waiting on the deck. His face is obscured, not quite in focus, though you gather that it is kind, and calming, and luminous. This figure is holding out his hand, inviting you to come aboard and join him on a magnificent journey.

As you step aboard, you recognize immediately that you have just taken the hand of God—the hand of love, and compassion, and infinite possibility.

Peer into the face of God. You're looking at yourself, the face of your divine, eternal spirit. A mirror is produced and held up to you. Behold that same image, powerful and exultant, a being of radiance and stillness and nobility, an adventurer on the cusp of an incredible journey now walking confidently past his crew toward the bridge to take his familiar place at the helm.

Feel the smooth, dark wood of the ship's wheel. Feel it warm to the touch of your hands. Feel that same warmth radiate outward into all the wood of the bridge, and then fill every quarter of the ship, and then diffuse into all the water in the sea.

You are that warmth.

Take this feeling with you as you head out into your life's adventure, a voyage which begins the moment you choose to weigh anchor. Trust the water to carry your vessel, and the wind to take you safely past the shoals and reefs of the bay into the open possibilities of the rest of your eternal life. Trust the captain of this vessel to sail steadily toward that glowing horizon of your magnificent future.

Trust him. Trust her.

Have faith in this force that takes on the names of everything it touches, this ageless spirit placing a single finger to the ground to identify the center of the world, this god in the shape of you, dressed like an admiral.

About the Author

Angelica Crystal Powers was born on her father's jet as it flew over the Alps above the border of Italy and France, and so—though raised in Italy—she considers both countries her native home. Her father, an inventor and entrepreneur, and mother, a ballet teacher and model, always encouraged Angelica to be independent and travel the journey of her choosing. And so, at the age of seventeen, she abandoned a life of privilege and travelled the world in search of spiritual discovery, a three-year journey that took her through the Middle East, Europe, China, Japan and the mountains of Nepal and India. A Master of Mind Potentiality and spiritual guide, A.C. Powers is now regarded as the "master of masters" in the techniques of attraction, imparting her knowledge to students around the world.

CPSIA information can be obtained at www.ICGtesting.com
Printed in the USA
LVOW081727200412

278511LV00001B/99/P